Jean Sasson lived in Saudi Arabia for over ten years from 1978 and became, during that time, the intimate friend and confidante of 'Sultana', who asked her to tell her story. Jean Sasson did so by writing *Princess* and *Daughters of Arabia,* both of which became international bestsellers. She now lives in her native southern USA.

Also by Jean Sasson

PRINCESS
DAUGHTERS OF ARABIA
THE RAPE OF KUWAIT

DESERT ROYAL

Jean Sasson

BANTAM BOOKS

LONDON • NEW YORK • TORONTO • SYDNEY • AUCKLAND

DESERT ROYAL
A BANTAM BOOK : 0 553 81218 1

Originally published in Great Britain by Doubleday,
a division of Transworld Publishers

PRINTING HISTORY
Doubleday edition published 1999
Bantam Books edition published 2000

3 5 7 9 10 8 6 4

Set in 11/12pt Sabon by Kestrel Data, Exeter, Devon

Bantam Books are published by Transworld Publishers, 61–63 Uxbridge Road, London W5 5SA, a division of The Random House Group Ltd, in Australia by Random House Australia (Pty) Ltd, 20 Alfred Street, Milsons Point, Sydney, NSW 2061, Australia, in New Zealand by Random House New Zealand Ltd, 18 Poland Road, Glenfield, Auckland 10, New Zealand and in South Africa by Random House (Pty) Ltd, Endulini, 5a Jubilee Road, Parktown 2193, South Africa.

Printed and bound in Germany by
Elsnerdruck, Berlin.

To Kayleigh

Contents

Author's Note

On 7 September, 1978 I travelled to Saudi Arabia with the idea that I would live and work in the country for only a few years, but I remained in Riyadh, the capital of that desert kingdom, until 1991.

In 1983 I met Sultana Al Sa'ud, a royal princess. This delightful woman exercised upon me a fascination that has not left me since.

I worked at the King Faisal Specialist Hospital and Research Centre for four years. During that time I met various members of the large Saudi royal family and made the sad discovery that on the whole they were spoiled and self-absorbed. Most could see no further than the monarchy and all its trappings.

However, Sultana was unlike any royal I had met. She was young and beautiful. Her dark hair fell over her shoulders and her eyes sparkled with curiosity. Her lips frequently opened wide in spontaneous laughter. Dressed in expensive clothes and decorated with eye-catching jewels, Sultana captured the undivided attention of everyone around her.

Beyond her obvious beauty and charm, I had

expected this royal to be like every other princess I had met, but I was both surprised and pleased to learn that Sultana was a woman with an independent mind who seemed to hunger to bring change to the lives of women in Saudi Arabia. Although she had been raised with the privileges of the enormously wealthy ruling family of Saudi Arabia, she made no effort to conceal that where issues regarding women were involved she was in a rebellion against the traditions and customs of her own country.

As our friendship slowly developed, I came to know a woman of great strength of will and character. Although her judgement and conduct is often clouded with passion, frequently creating emotional situations unexpected among adults, it is easy to overlook such behaviour, for Sultana is selfless, caring and sensitive when it comes to other women. When she discovers any injustice against another woman she springs into action, regardless of personal danger to herself.

When Sultana confided to me that she had conceived many plans to make the tragic stories of Saudi women known to the world, but had never been free to do so because of the danger it would attract to her immediate family and herself, I agreed to help her make her wish come true. Together, we would bring these horrifying and unbelievable true stories to the world's attention.

And so, protecting her anonymity, I became the voice for a princess.

In the book, *Princess*, the world first learned of Sultana's life as an unwanted daughter of a cruel man in an unforgiving society that places little value on females. Sultana's most beloved sister,

Sara, was married against her will to a much older man whom she did not know or love. From the time of her wedding, Sara was subjected to terrible sexual assaults by her husband. Only after Sara attempted suicide did her father allow her to seek a divorce and return home.

Sultana's own unhappy childhood experiences caused her to become a rebellious teenager. But she learned in a most horrifying manner that rebellion against the harsh system of her country could only lead to disaster when one of her friends was *executed* by her own father, for the 'crime' of sexual misconduct.

At the age of sixteen, Sultana was told by her father that he had arranged for her to marry a cousin, Kareem. Sultana and Kareem's betrothal was unlike most Saudi engagements, for Kareem requested to meet his future bride, and his request was granted. Upon their first meeting, Kareem and Sultana were strongly attracted to each other. They quickly fell in love, and enjoyed a special union of mutual love, so unlike most Saudi marriages.

The early years of her marriage brought Sultana the tranquillity she had always desired. She and Kareem were blessed first with a son, Abdullah, and then with two daughters, Maha and Amani.

Sultana and her family remained in Riyadh during the Gulf War of 1991. The princess was saddened that this war, rather than helping the status of women in Saudi Arabia as she had hoped, made their lives even more difficult. Sultana mourned that when the war ended, 'thin veils thickened, bare ankles were covered, and loosened chains were tightened'.

In *Daughters of Arabia*, the princess and I told the world that her immediate family had learned that she was the princess behind the book *Princess*, which had become a bestseller in many countries, but that the secret of her identity had been maintained as far as the rest of the royal family was concerned. Readers also learned that despite Sultana's constant battle against the status quo, and her own relatively enlightened marriage, her own two daughters did not escape the pressures of feudal prejudices against women in Saudi Arabia.

Sultana's daughters each reacted differently to their Saudi heritage. Her elder daughter, Maha, hated the life of a woman in Saudi Arabia, and following in Sultana's own path she rebelled against the injustices she saw inflicted on women in her country. She became so unsettled in her mind that she had to undergo psychiatric treatment in London before she could resume life in Saudi Arabia.

Amani, Sultana's younger daughter, reacted in a way which was even more troubling to her mother. Amani embraced the Islamic faith with a distressing degree of fanaticism. As Sultana fights *against* the veil, Amani battles *for* the veil.

In this third book, Sultana has asked me to be her voice once more. Although she continues to challenge the treatment of women in Saudi Arabia by letting the world know that the ongoing abuse of women in her country is both alarming and routine, Sultana has discovered a new direction for helping women worldwide, and persists in her gallant crusade for reform.

Although readers of this book will learn that

Sultana is far from perfect, and that her imperfections are often all too human, no-one can doubt her sincerity when it comes to fighting for the rights of women.

As a writer, and her friend, I am proud to tell the story of this extraordinary princess.

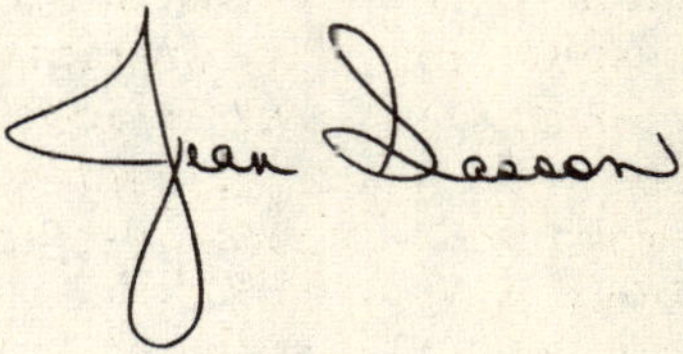

My Dream

A few months ago as I lay sleeping, my beloved mother came to me in a dream. Mother was robed in an embroidered cloak of vivid red; her long black hair was braided with golden threads. Her face was shining and unlined, and her luminous eyes were all-knowing and wise.

Her appearance under a shimmering green tree beside a spring of the bluest water dazzled me. Bright flowers grew lush and abundant all around her.

In my dream my heart was beating wildly as I called out, 'Mother!' With arms outspread I anxiously hurried towards her. But an invisible barrier kept her tantalizingly out of reach.

Mother gazed at the youngest of her earthly children with great love mingled with sad resignation.

And then she spoke. Although her voice was sonorous and sweet, her revelation was stern. 'Sultana,' she said, 'my journey here has been frustrated by your pains, discontents, disappointments and misfortunes.' She quietly scrutinized me.

'Daughter, when you were a wayward child I often had to frighten you into reasonable behaviour.' She arched her eyebrows. 'I see that my presence is still needed, Sultana.'

The knowledge that I had created worries for my mother, even after she had entered paradise, caused me to burst into tears.

I was born a princess in a rich desert kingdom where the persecution of women is increasing, and I could not dispute that I have led an unconventional life.

I cried out, 'Mother, a great wind has carried me through life! How might I have lived my life differently?'

Mother slowly shook her head. 'Even in the midst of a heated battle, Sultana, a good heart fights clean.'

I flinched.

Mother's look softened. 'But that is not the matter of which I am now speaking, child.'

'Then, what?' I entreated.

'Sultana, your life is as that of a mindless magician unfurling endless silks. You seem to have everything in life; yet you have nothing. Your existence does not bring you happiness, my daughter.'

Desperate for Mother to comfort me as she had done in the past, the significance of her words slipped past me.

Then the fragile petals of the flowers around her began to fold, and Mother's countenance, too, began to fade.

I cried out, 'Mother! Please stay! Wait!'

Her incandescent form was now barely visible, yet I clearly heard her say, 'Sultana, in the middle of a feast you are starving. Dissolve into something greater than yourself, my child.'

I emerged from that dream in an ecstasy of joy, but the memory of Mother's mysterious message has continued to haunt me.

Sadly, I had to acknowledge that Mother's words were true, that I had let my life stagnate. Once, I embarked on a noble and stimulating quest to improve the lives of women in my land. But finding myself helpless against the unassailable power of Saudi Arabian men, I had let myself grow discouraged. Yet, so long as women in my own country can be married against their will, physically abused and raped under the sanction of the law, even legally murdered at the whim of their fathers, husbands and brothers, how could I stop fighting?

Following my mother's visit, I took courage from the knowledge that there was still a purpose for me in this ongoing struggle, a new role that I was meant to fulfil. At this moment, however, I had no understanding of where that might lead.

Munira's Destiny

One of the major traditions of Islam is reported to have originated from a meeting of the Prophet Mohammed and his followers when the Prophet took a stick and wrote on the ground, 'There is not one among you whose sitting place is not written by God, whether in fire or in paradise.' From this tradition, the Islamic faith teaches that all things in life are predestined and that every person's fate has been decreed by Allah. While this fatalism creates a dignified resignation to life's hardships for many Muslims, I have fought against this pessimistic inertia throughout my life, and I cannot accept the tragic lives lived by so many Saudi women as the preordained will of Allah.

So when I learned that a dreadful piece of our family history was about to be repeated, I knew that I could never just fatalistically accept a horrifying and shameful destiny being assigned to one of my nieces.

Our family had recently returned to our palace in Riyadh from a trip to Egypt. My husband Kareem and our eldest child and only son Abdullah were in Kareem's home office. Amani, our youngest daughter, was in the garden with her pets, and I was sitting in the living room with our elder daughter, Maha.

Suddenly, my sister Sara, and three of her four daughters – Fadeela, Nashwa and Sahar – burst through the door.

I rose with a smile to greet my most beloved sister, but I saw the fear shining through Sara's gaze. Her dark eyes desperately sought mine as she clasped my hands. She told me to sit down, that she had appalling news.

'What is wrong, Sara?'

Sara's melodious voice betrayed a great bitterness. 'Sultana, while you were away, Ali arranged for Munira to be married. The wedding is ten days from tomorrow.'

Maha grabbed my hand from Sara's, and dug her nails into my palm. 'Oh, Mother, no!'

I pulled away. My hands twitched nervously as I spread my fingers across my face. One idea beat mercilessly into my brain. Another young woman, my own flesh and blood, to be married against her will.

Munira was the oldest daughter of my despised brother, Ali. She was a pretty, though slight girl, who appeared many years younger than her true age. Munira had always been an obedient child whose timid demeanour aroused our sympathies and affection.

Munira's mother was Ali's first wife, Tammam, the royal cousin my brother had married so many years before. At the time, Ali had readily boasted that his marriage to Tammam was for the sole purpose of sexual release when he came home to our country in between school terms abroad. Love and affection were never on his agenda.

Anyone could have easily predicted Tammam's miserable future. She had been married while still a child, and she never had an opportunity to develop emotionally. Even as a mature woman, Tammam rarely entered into conversation, and when she did speak, her voice was so low the listener was forced to lean close to hear her.

Three years after his marriage to Tammam, Ali took a second wife. Since Tammam was a most dutiful wife, Ali was questioned by our eldest sister, Nura, as to his need for a second spouse. She later revealed to us that Ali had declared that his displeasure was linked to Tammam's unhappiness. He was angry and baffled over the fact that his young bride had become a melancholy wife. With the greatest puzzlement, Ali claimed that Tammam had not *once smiled* since the day he had become her husband!

Tammam's union with Ali produced three children, two daughters and a son. The daughters were as cheerless as their mother, while the son was a perfect arrogant duplicate of his father. By now, their ranks had been swelled by twelve other children, by a total of six women apart from Tammam.

Munira had lived a troubled and unhappy life. As the daughter of a man who cared little for daughters, she had spent her early years striving to win the love of her father, a man who had no love to give. In that respect, Munira's childhood quest for a father's love resembled my own. But that is where the similarity ended. At least I had survived the deprivation of my father's love with my ability to love intact. Munira's thwarted love for her father gradually twisted into open dislike before turning into a combination of fear and hatred. Those feelings had now grown to include all men – even those men who were kind. Five years before, at age sixteen, Munira had told her mother that she wished to remain celibate.

And so, unlike most Saudi girls, who spend much of their youth perfecting methods to keep their future husbands content, Munira determined a different life for herself. She trained as a social worker, intending to spend her life assisting the handicapped who are so scorned in our land. Nevertheless, she made it clear that she would only attend to the female handicapped.

For a period of time it appeared that Ali had simply forgotten the fact that his eldest daughter was unwed. But, sadly, he had been reminded of her single state during a recent family social event. Now Ali was denying his daughter the one pleasure she sought, which was to be allowed to remain unmarried.

The moment a girl is born in Arab lands, the parents immediately begin to think of an appropriate marriage. With the idea of future allegiances, suitable families with eligible sons are studied keenly. While a Saudi girl remains unmarried, she must stay a virgin. On the other hand, virginity prolonged is deemed a family disgrace. Now that Munira had turned twenty-one years old, her unmarried state was causing her father grave discomfort.

Maha interrupted my thoughts. She loved her cousin and knew Munira's views on marriage. 'Mother! Uncle Ali can't force Munira to marry, can he?'

'To whom is Munira promised?' I sputtered.

Sara hesitated so long that I thought she did not know the answer. Finally, she said, with a long sigh, 'Sultana, Munira is to wed Hadi.'

My memory was barren of a face to connect with the name. 'Hadi? Who?'

'*The* Hadi. Sultana, don't you remember? Ali's boyhood friend who travelled with our family to Cairo.'

I could barely speak. '*That* Hadi?'

Sara nodded woefully. 'Yes. That Hadi.'

The memory of our shared traumatic experience slammed down between us. In disbelief, I stared into my sister's eyes.

'No. No,' was all that I could utter.

'Who *is* this Hadi?' Maha demanded.

Who, indeed? Where was I to begin?

I mumbled. 'He's Ali's friend from childhood, daughter. You do not know of him.'

Sara settled closer to me and her hands sought mine. We continued to gaze into each other's eyes. Our thoughts were in unison. Sara was reliving the most traumatic time of her life.

More than twenty years before, against her will, Sara had been wed to a much older man, a man who had sexually abused her from the first moment of their union. It was only after Sara's attempted suicide that our mother had managed to convince our father to allow her to divorce. Despite her return to our family home, my dear sister had been unable to shake off a chronic and debilitating depression.

During this same period of time, our eldest sister Nura and her husband Ahmed were in the process of building a new palace. Nura planned to travel to Italy to purchase furnishings for this home, and, along the way, to visit Cairo.

Much to my surprise and delight, Nura and Ahmed invited both Sara and me to accompany them and their children on the trip. Every coin has two sides, and my happiness was soon tempered when father decided that my brother, Ali, and his friend, Hadi, would also be a part of our entourage. Despite this distressing and dispiriting news, we went along on the trip.

While we were in Cairo, Sara and I were astounded to discover that our brother's friend was even more obnoxious than Ali! Neither of us had imagined that such a thing was possible. We soon learned that in comparison to the spoiled and difficult Ali, Hadi was pure evil.

Although a student at the Religious Institute, which was a boys' school in Riyadh for training *mutawwas*, or men of religion, Hadi had absorbed none of the goodness called for in our Holy Koran. His black soul remained untouched by his religious education.

Hadi hated women with a purposeful vengeance, and often expressed his opinion that all young girls should be wed at the first sign of their menses. In Hadi's mind, women were on this earth for three purposes: to provide for a man's sexual pleasure, to serve a man, and to bear a man's children.

Of course, Hadi thought that Sara and I were uncontrollable females, and often said so. If he had been the master of our destinies, Sara and I were convinced that we would have been stoned to death, and that Hadi would have been there to throw the first stone!

Despite his expressed hatred of the female

gender, Hadi was keen to have sex with as many different women as possible. And on that trip to Cairo and Italy, he had done just that. Most disturbing of all, Ali had joined Hadi in his perverse behaviour! While in Cairo, Sara and I had inadvertently come upon Hadi and Ali sexually assaulting a girl who was no more than eight years old! The scene had been one of horror and violence, and neither Sara nor I had ever forgotten the haunting images of what we saw that day.

Certain that such an evil boy would have grown into an evil man, we were now filled with panic at the thought that such a person would soon have absolute control over a dear and sweet child unprepared to defend herself.

Sobbing, I fell into Sara's arms. Our tears were so contagious that our daughters began sobbing with us.

The sound of our anguished cries evidently reached Kareem's office, for he and Abdullah soon came rushing into the room.

Full of concern, Kareem pulled me away from my sister. 'Sultana! Sara! Whatever has happened?'

And Abdullah demanded of his sister Maha, 'Who has died?'

I stammered through my wails, 'Death would be better!'

Kareem was becoming increasingly alarmed. 'What? What?'

Maha spoke up. 'It's about cousin Munira, Father. Uncle Ali has arranged her marriage.'

Even Kareem was sobered by that news. Every member of our extended family knew of Munira's repulsion for men and marriage.

Unlike many Saudi males, my husband was not a man who believed in force when it came to marriage. Kareem and I had agreed many years before that our daughters should be educated before marriage and that, when the time came for them to be wed, they would have the right to choose their own husbands. Never would Maha or Amani have to face Munira's grim situation. Indeed, our religion forbids the forcing of females into a union not of their liking, but, like much that is good in our Islamic faith, this is misinterpreted or simply ignored.

'Who is she to wed?' Kareem asked loudly to make himself heard over the sound of sobbing women.

'You will never believe it,' I sighed.

'It is a great disaster,' Sara added, dabbing at the tears flowing down her cheeks.

'Tell me, who?'

I gazed up at Kareem with sorrow. 'Ali is going to wed his daughter to an old friend.'

'Old in *years*?' Kareem questioned with a grimace.

'Two ways old,' I said. 'An old friend, who is old!'

An exasperated Kareem said, 'Please, Sultana! Don't make me guess.'

Sara could sit still no longer. She rose to her feet, wailing. 'It's *Hadi* . . . Ali's friend from many years ago. The detested Hadi!'

My husband's face turned white. His eyes grew fierce and his voice was disbelieving. '*Hadi, from the Egyptian trip?*'

'That very Hadi!'

'Oh! This will never do.' Kareem looked at his

son. 'Abdullah, I must speak with Ali at once. We'll reschedule our morning meeting.'

Abdullah nodded solemnly.

While Ali was a friend of Hadi's, none of Ali's brothers-in-law claimed a relationship with the man. He was so thoroughly disliked that everyone kept a distance from him, except Ali. Only Ali was able to find admirable qualities in Hadi. He was certainly not a part of our small coterie of close relatives and friends.

Although schooled as a man of religion, Hadi now made his living working for the Saudi government. As a friend of a high-ranking prince, he had manoeuvred himself into a perfect position to become fabulously wealthy.

Due to his excellent financial prospects those who did not know his wicked disposition might consider him an eligible and desirable husband. But two of my sisters-in-law were acquainted with Hadi's three wives, and they had heard that his evil nature had grown rather than lessened. It was enough to know that Hadi was secretly named 'Satan's most favoured son' by the women he had wed.

With Kareem's words I felt a small flicker of hope. While I knew that Ali's sisters could never have the slightest influence on him, if the men of our family took action, perhaps poor Munira could be saved from a destiny she surely would consider worse than instantaneous death.

'When will you see Ali?'

'Tomorrow.'

'Asad will go with you,' Sara promised. 'And I'll telephone Nura. Perhaps Ahmed will go with you, too. This marriage must be stopped!'

With such plans under way, I felt somewhat relieved.

Kareem and I were so physically and emotionally exhausted by this family drama that we slept that night without our usual loving embrace.

Early the next morning, I lay in bed wondering what the day might bring, while Kareem took his morning shower. Since I feared that Kareem might forget to tell me some important points in his talk with my brother, I was trying to think of a way that I might listen in on their conversation.

When Kareem went into the adjoining sitting room to telephone my brother, I slipped the receiver from the phone by the bed and listened to their call. I heard them agree to meet at the palace of Tammam, where Ali was taking Kareem's call. Obviously, Ali had spent the previous evening with his first wife.

I rushed into Maha's room and said, 'Dress quickly! We are going to visit your Auntie Tammam and Munira. They need us.'

When I told Kareem that Maha and I were leaving to visit Tammam and Munira, I saw a line of worry crease his forehead. 'Sultana, if you and Maha wish to visit Tammam and Munira, I will not stop you. But, take care and promise that you will not intrude on my meeting with your brother.'

Full of innocence, I gave my word that I would not disrupt their talk. But Kareem had not requested that I promise not to listen in on them.

Tammam was not expecting us, but she seemed pleased to have visitors and was very gracious. After greeting her auntie, Maha went directly to the room of her cousin, Munira.

Prior to Kareem's arrival, I convinced Tammam

that it was in our best interest to sit quietly in the banquet hall adjacent to Ali's sitting room. 'We might be summoned,' I told her.

As soon as we entered the large room, I began to rummage through the contents of my large handbag. I had learned many years ago that to request permission for whatever unconventional action I might take would open the door for a negative response. Therefore, I now simply act and let others react.

Tammam's jaw dropped but she was too timid to protest when I took an electronic device out of my purse and inserted the small listening-aid into my right ear. I smiled at the astonished Tammam, and said, 'Who knows what men are plotting against good women?'

I had purchased this device several years before at a specialty shop in New York City, which stocked an amazing variety of spying devices, after having seen their advertisement in a hotel guest-information book. At that time in my life, it had been of the utmost importance to closely follow the secret activities of Amani. Fearing she might bring harm to herself through her extreme religious fervour, I had felt compelled to spy on my youngest child. But I soon became bored with her endless conversations regarding detailed aspects of our religious faith, and I had put away the listening device. However, earlier that morning, before leaving for Ali's house, I had remembered the contraption, and had come prepared to eavesdrop on the all-powerful men who ruled our lives.

I fiddled with the gadget for a few moments. Past experience had shown me that, even if the mechanism did not work perfectly, it did greatly amplify voices coming from adjoining rooms.

I gave Tammam a reassuring smile, but I could see that she was fearful. My sister-in-law sat like one stricken dumb, her hands cupped over her mouth.

Unintentionally, I had placed the volume level to its highest point, so when in the next room Kareem, Asad and Ahmed loudly greeted Ali, my feet left the floor, throwing my body against the wall.

Tammam gave a small shriek of alarm.

After I had gathered my wits, I held my finger to my lips.

Thankfully, the men's prolonged greetings were so boisterous that they had heard nothing amiss.

I smiled as I listened. I had always taken the greatest secret pleasure in listening to forbidden conversations.

The four men spent long, silent moments preparing their tea to their liking. When they finally did speak, their conversation dwelt on unimportant matters. After everyone's health was assured, there was talk of various business matters. Their talk lingered for a long time on the declining health of the King. Uncle Fahd is my own immediate family's leader of choice, and there is great dread of the day he will no longer rule.

I was getting impatient when Ahmed finally approached the subject that had really brought them together.

'Ali, we hear news that Munira is to be married.'

There was a short pause. Then Ali rang a bell

for one of his servants to go and fetch some freshly baked pastries to accompany his tea.

I presumed that my brother was playing for time to deliberate his response to such an unexpected question. Still, it is true that my brother does eat to excess. Much to my amusement, he was getting wider by the year.

The listening device was functioning so efficiently that I soon heard the smacking of Ali's full lips as he devoured one honey-laced pastry after another. The other men sat in silence.

Finally, his appetite satiated, Ali was ready to respond to Ahmed's question. 'Yes. You are correct, Ahmed. Munira is at the age to be wed. And, I have found a good match.' He hesitated before adding, 'Surely Tammam has notified my sisters of the date for the wedding celebration.'

Kareem cleared his throat, then began speaking tentatively. 'Ali, consider us as your brothers. And, as brothers, we are here to support you in whatever decisions you might make – on any matter.'

'That is true,' Asad said promptly.

Kareem continued with great tact. 'Ali, the zig-zag of human life is so puzzling. I wonder if you have shone the torch of light on Munira's particular character, or on the age of the man she is to wed.'

Ahmed was the one who finally came to the point. 'Is Munira not younger than some of Hadi's own children?'

There was perfect silence.

Asad hurriedly suggested, 'If Munira must wed, is there not another nearer her age who would be more to her liking?'

Undoubtedly, Ali was not pleased by this highly unusual interference in his private business. Still, he must have felt himself ensnared, for he made a surprising concession. 'I will let Munira decide!'

I held my hands over my mouth to keep from creating a commotion. Once I could control myself, I motioned to Tammam, and held both hands over my head and then towards the ground, as a signal that I was praying and praising Allah.

Dull-witted Tammam looked at me with a bewildered expression. She seemed to think that I was telling her it was time for the noon prayer, for she glanced at her watch and shook her head back and forth, no.

In a slow, measured whisper I mouthed to her, 'Ali is to let Munira decide!'

Tammam smiled meekly.

For the first time ever I felt a twinge of sympathy for Ali. Tammam was such a spineless creature! Were I the mother of Munira, I would have great difficulty in suppressing my joy at this news. Charitably, I decided her emotions had been permanently dulled by years of maltreatment.

'I will call Munira now,' Ali said decisively. I heard the sound of his muffled footsteps as the door opened and closed.

While Ali was absent, the three waiting men turned to small talk regarding our recent Egyptian holiday. I felt a flicker of disappointment since I was hoping that they would discuss some confidential family business that I did not know, but not so confidential that I could not repeat it.

Soon I heard Ali re-enter the room. His booming

voice sounded self-assured. 'Munira, your uncles love and esteem you greatly. They have taken precious time from their busy schedules to personally deliver congratulations for your up-coming marriage.'

Kareem, Asad and Ahmed murmured quietly, but Munira said nothing in reply.

Knowing Munira's dread of men, I suspected that the poor girl was so overwhelmed by the male attention directed towards her that she was struck dumb.

Ali continued, 'Munira, child, the man Hadi has asked that you become an adored wife. You are aware of his friendship with this family and of his ability to provide for you and any children you might have. I have sought permission from Almighty God to give you in wedlock to Hadi. Tell me now, Munira, if you approve.'

I waited for Munira's words. And waited. And waited.

'Munira?'

Silence.

Ali spoke in an exhilarated tone, 'God is great! Munira's silence signifies her approval!' He laughed heartily. 'Go, return to your room, child, and know that your modesty in this matter has made your father very happy.'

I felt numbness creep into my face and spread throughout my body. I realized that Ali had cunningly used a sly trick to close the mouths of his male kin. He had repeated nearly word for word what Prophet Mohammed had asked his own daughter, Fatima, when he had arranged for her to marry a cousin, Imam Ali. When Fatima made no response, all good Muslims know that the Prophet interpreted the girl's refusal to answer as a sign of great modesty.

The door slammed.

Under the circumstances, my husband and brothers-in-law could say no more. If they did, they would be arguing against the Holy Prophet!

Ali thanked them profusely. 'Your concern for my family has lightened my heart! I am a most fortunate man! Please, come again soon.'

As the men left, the door slammed once more. I heard my brother's self-satisfied chuckle.

With a tormented moan, I slumped against the wall. What had happened? Had Ali threatened Munira during their short walk through his palace? Or had the terrorized Munira simply gone mute?

With tears coursing down my cheeks, I looked at Tammam and slowly shook my head. All was lost!

As a woman who had never known the power of hope, Tammam didn't appear surprised or upset. She rose to her feet and came and stood by my side. I wept while she comforted me.

Within moments the door burst open. We had been discovered by Ali! My brother pulled himself up to his full height as he glared at his wife and sister.

I glared back at him. Disgust swept over me. Surely, today, my brother was physically uglier than I had ever seen him. His figure had taken on a roundness visible even under his *thobe*. He wore a new pair of horn-rimmed glasses with thick lenses that made his eyes appear shockingly large.

Our dislike for each other was mutual. Our

childhood experiences had created great distances between us that will never be overcome. At this moment, the hatred between my brother and me was so thick that I imagined the room growing darker around me.

Defiant, I spoke with venom dripping from my tongue, 'Ah, my wicked brother! For sure, Judgement Day will not be to your liking.'

Tammam's sallow face collapsed in fright, and she shrank back in horror at my effrontery. Evidently, she never stood up to her husband. The poor woman tried to apologize for my words – only the words of another lowly woman – but Ali cut short her apology with a dismissive flick of his hand.

It's little wonder he does not love her, I thought cruelly. No man could respect one so cowardly.

As I watched Ali's face, I knew that he was searching through his mind for a remark that would wound me. Many were the times I had got the better of my brother with words. He had never been particularly quick verbally, and now he appeared even more lost for words.

I smirked, leaned back, and relaxed. When it came to a battle of wits, I could always outshine Ali. But suddenly he puffed out his hanging jowls. My disdainful sneer slowly began to fade. Had Ali realized, as had I, that when one is the victor, there is no need for verbal repartee?

He began to laugh with relish. The sight of my cheerfully obese brother, standing there triumphant, knowing he was fully supported by the entrenched legal institutions of my country, caused me to sink to the floor in despair.

Munira's fate was settled, and I feared that there

was nothing I could do or say that would change the horror that awaited her.

Even after Ali closed the door and began his slow lumbering walk down the long corridor leading to the front entrance of the palace, I could hear the sound of his low, wicked laughter.

Munira's Wedding

The shock of failure in my confrontation with Ali meant that I went directly home and took to my bed. My head was throbbing severely, and I did not join my family for the evening meal.

Later that evening, when my distressed husband told me of the meeting with Ali, I did not confess that I already knew the outcome of the visit. When I began to cry, a sympathetic Kareem comforted me.

The following morning I was still so distraught that I remained in bed long after Kareem left our home for his offices in the city. As I lay in bed, my thoughts swirled around Munira and the terrifying and grim life she would soon lead. My sense of helplessness in the face of Munira's predicament brought forth a disturbing question: when it came to improving the lives of individual women, what accomplishments could Sultana Al Sa'ud really claim as her own?

Very little, up to this point, I had to admit. For the first time in my life, I was forced to acknowledge that my lofty aspirations to assist helpless women had come to nothing. My spirits sank so low at this bitter thought that I began to crave an alcoholic drink. I was longing for a drink even before I had my breakfast! Pushing aside any thought of food, I got out of bed and went straight to the bottle of scotch sitting on the bedroom credenza. After pouring myself a generous amount of the liquor, I took a long drink and waited for the expected warmth to flow through my body.

Suddenly I was struck with a second worry. During the past few months, my cravings for alcohol had grown. Would the solace I was receiving from alcohol now lead to a personal predicament? Was I becoming an alcoholic? Such an idea caused me to throw the glass to the floor. I moaned and covered my eyes with my hands.

From my childhood on, I had been taught that intoxicating spirits are evil and totally forbidden to Muslims. I still remember my mother telling me that Prophet Mohammed had cursed many men in connection with liquor. Mother said that our great prophet cursed the man who squeezed it, the one who carried it, the one to whom it was carried, the one who served it, the one who drank it, the one who dealt in it, the one who devoured its price, the one who purchased it, and the one from whom it was purchased. None were to be spared!

Yet, despite my mother's dire warning, somehow, I now found myself ensnared by the promise of fleeting happiness so easily found in a bottle of alcohol.

In the Al Sa'ud family I am not alone in this sin. Alcohol has taken a shocking toll on the lives of many of my royal cousins. To speak truthfully, I must say if these cousins are not buying or selling alcohol, they are drinking it. And, they do this, regardless of both religious taboo and the law.

What would our mother think?

Everyone who resides in the Kingdom of Saudi Arabia is fully aware that it is illegal to consume alcohol. It's common knowledge that every year there are a large number of Saudis as well as foreigners imprisoned for the offence of possessing or consuming alcohol. It is also well-known that such laws do not apply to members of the Al Sa'ud family. But, while the male members of the royal family remain unpunished for any crime they might commit, it's a different matter when it comes to Al Sa'ud females. We are saved from public condemnation for our missteps because of the embarrassment such an admission would cause our rulers, but female members of my family are forced to pay a high penalty should they develop any kind of addiction.

Returning to bed, I tried to count on my fingers all the female royal cousins who had become addicted to alcohol or to drugs, but I ran out of fingers. Within the past few years the problem has become so rampant that special clinics for substance abuse have begun opening within the kingdom. No longer is it necessary for Al Sa'ud men to send their alcohol- or drug-addicted wives abroad for rehabilitation.

Only a few months before, I had visited a cousin committed to one of these clinics. The atmosphere there was one of wealth and privilege. Soft steps and hushed voices told the visitor that they were in a medical facility like no other. The doctors and nurses were foreign, as were all the other staff. To ensure that they were never alone, each patient was assigned five personal nurses, all women who had grown accustomed to working with over-pampered royal princesses.

I had found my cousin in a large three-room suite where the luxuries of her normal life were duplicated. Special chefs created the finest food, which was served on costly china. My cousin continued to dress in expensive designer gowns while entertaining her closest friends and relatives in the clinic suites. The only accessories lacking in this new setting were alcohol and drugs.

Although her treatment consisted of many sessions with qualified physicians, she was not subjected to the humiliation – or the benefit – of group therapy, as are addicts in Western countries.

The cost for this special treatment at that clinic was over 100,000 Saudi riyals ($26,000) per week. My cousin remained in the facility for sixteen weeks, and was pronounced cured of her habit. Unfortunately, within a few months of being discharged, she once again resumed her addiction to alcohol. At last count, I heard this cousin has been treated at the special clinic on at least five occasions.

Yet, once admitted for such treatment, whether cured or not, nothing is ever the same again for the unfortunate Saudi wife. Servants gossip to other servants, and the truth always escapes. The addicted princess is looked upon with great pity by her female cousins, but her husband will usually reject her, possibly taking a second wife or even seeking divorce. As every Saudi woman knows, divorce brings the loss of everything – status and children. A divorced woman soon becomes socially isolated and ostracized.

Recently, Hazrat Al Sa'ud, another royal cousin afflicted with alcoholism, had been divorced by her husband. Her five young children, who now lived with their father and his other two wives, had been forbidden all contact with Hazrat. Her own blood family had renounced her as well, and she now lived under the supervision of an elderly, blind aunt and two Filipino servants. Yet the attraction to alcohol was so strong that Hazrat still took reckless chances at every opportunity in order to acquire the drink that had brought about her ruin.

Only a week before, my eldest sister Nura had been told that Hazrat had caused an explosion when trying to concoct homemade wine out of grape juice, sugar and yeast. Nura said that Hazrat's elderly aunt swore the explosion was so loud that she thought the Iraqis were bombing Riyadh. She took cover under a bed and remained there until she heard Hazrat wailing and weeping over the lost liquor. There was no denying that Hazrat's life was utterly ruined by the very craving for alcohol that I was now experiencing.

I shuddered. Fearful of what my future might hold if my secret was ever exposed, I promised myself that Kareem must never know that I was consuming alcohol in the morning hours. I had understood long ago that my strength and boldness were the arrows that had pierced my husband's heart and drawn him to me. Surely the foundation on which our love was based would crumble should Kareem discover my weakness.

Horrified at the turn my life had taken, I vowed that I would overcome this progressive and dangerous desire for alcohol. I began to recite the ninety-nine names of Allah aloud, hoping that, by proving my devoutness, the God of all Muslims would take pity on me, and give me added strength to defeat my weakness. My lips moved as I whispered the words, 'The Compassionate, The Merciful, The Sovereign, The Holy, The Giver of Peace, The Protector, The Mighty One, The Creator, The Majestic, The Great Forgiver—'

My sincere devotions were interrupted by an hysterical Maha. My daughter said that Munira had just telephoned in tears. The poor girl had confirmed to Maha what I had already expected; that she had good reason for her silence on the day her uncles had visited. Munira said that Ali had threatened to beat both her mother and herself if she dared to open her mouth in protest about her engagement to Hadi.

Poor Munira also confided that her daily prayers now consisted of pleas to God for an early death before her wedding date.

It was then that memories of Sara's attempted suicide caused me to rise from my bed. Consulting with Maha, I discarded one risky proposal to rescue the bride after another. Finally, we concluded that a simple plan was best. We decided to hide Munira in our home at Jeddah until Hadi became so mortified by the reluctance of his young bride that he would nullify their engagement.

I eagerly telephoned Sara and told her to come quickly. I was hoping that I could induce my most intelligent sister to join us in devising further strategy.

When Sara arrived, she bewildered me when she balked at the idea, even warning me that she felt compelled to alert Kareem of my reckless objective.

'Sara!' I admonished. 'You once travelled the same path as poor Munira. Do your own memories of abuse not compel you to help save this girl?'

Sara appeared frozen in place.

'Sara?'

Sara's brooding face belied the calm tone of her voice. 'Sultana,' she confessed, 'every day of my life is clouded by what happened during that time. Even when I am most happy with Asad, a sliver of pain always works its way into my consciousness.' She paused briefly. 'If I could save Munira from such a fate, I would do it. But only God can save Munira, Sultana. Only God.'

'God gave women cunning minds in order to scheme,' I argued. 'How else can we defeat the evil nature of men?'

Sara placed a light hand on my shoulder. 'You may have the years of a woman on you, my sister, but in many ways, you are still a child.'

I turned away, so disappointed and angry that I could not speak.

'Come, Sultana. Try to think clearly for one moment, and you will realize that anything you might do to conceal Munira will only serve to make our brother, and Hadi, even more determined. If you hide Munira, they will find her. Then, Hadi will marry her anyway, but by that time his heart will be filled with anger and bitterness. Her life will only be worsened by your efforts.'

Like the caged bird that finally comes to acceptance of its captivity, the lightness of hope left me. I collapsed on the sofa and wrapped my arms around my body. Sara spoke the truth, so, for now, I put aside all thoughts of extricating my niece. I knew that excluding a miracle, Munira would be Hadi's future wife. And there was nothing any of us could do about it.

After Sara departed for her own home, I returned to my bed and spent the rest of the day lethargic with hopelessness.

Nine days passed as fleetingly as mere moments. The evening of Munira's wedding arrived, all too soon.

Although Ali possessed no love for his eldest daughter, his position as a high-ranking prince ensured that Munira's wedding would be a grandiose occasion. The celebration and wedding were to take place at the King Faisal Hall, a large building in Riyadh where many Saudi royal weddings have been staged.

On the night of the wedding, a stream of limousines wove their way to the entrance of the hall, discharging flocks of veiled women. Our driver stopped at the wide steps that led to the entrance of the building. Two doormen rushed to open the doors of our automobile, and my daughters and I stepped out into a night filled with music. I could feel the beat of Arabic dancing music drifting through the hall as we moved towards the stairs.

Although we were all veiled, I knew that most of the other guests were members of the royal family, or women whose families had close connections with our family.

Other than the groom, his father or brother, the father of the bride, and possibly a *mutawwa*, or religious man, we never see men at this kind of occasion. Men and women in my country celebrate weddings at separate locations. Even as we women were gathering at the King Faisal Hall, our men were congregating at Ali's Riyadh palace.

As my daughters and I walked across the threshold into the large hall, a swarm of female servants dressed exactly alike in red velvet gowns and caps waited to relieve us of our cloaks and veils. The three of us were elaborately dressed in expensive designer gowns that we had purchased the year before while holidaying in Paris. I wore a black evening dress covered in red Italian lace.

A few days earlier, in an attempt to distract me from Munira's plight, Kareem had sent a trusted Lebanese employee on one of our private planes to Paris for the sole purpose of acquiring a special gift for me. The ten-tiered diamond choker was now fastened securely around my neck.

Maha was arrayed in a lovely burgundy silk dress that draped loosely off her broad shoulders. A diamond and pearl necklace shaped in the form of simple teardrops covered the smooth flesh of her neckline. While selecting her jewelry, Maha had whispered that she thought it appropriate that even her jewels appeared to weep for her dear cousin.

Amani was fitted out in a dark blue gown with a matching jacket. In keeping with her strict religious beliefs, she had chosen a garment most severe in style that covered her up to the neck.

Since our faith regards the love of jewelry and ornaments as natural and becoming for a woman, if they are not used to attract men and arouse their sexual desires, Amani could hardly object to my wishes that she wear beautiful jewels that night. I had reminded my pious daughter of what she already knew – other than Hadi, his attendant, her Uncle Ali and a man of religion, no men would be present at our gathering. Once she agreed that her faith did permit her to wear precious stones free of guilt, Amani selected a charming ruby-and-diamond necklace which had been cleverly fashioned to resemble a cluster of sparkling flowers.

Both my daughters were lovely, and on any other occasion, I would have been proud to display them.

When Maha and Amani joined female cousins near their own age, I left them and wandered alone into the vast hall.

The music was so loud and the singer so shrill that I could only liken the sound to shrieks of terror! Or was this just my imagination?

I winced. A pillar of light shone overhead. Such an over-abundance of lighting had created a blinding effect. At Ali's behest, special decorators flown in from Egypt had covered the entire surface of the ceiling with brightly coloured lights. Looking around the room, I was astonished at the gaudiness of the decorations. The room was steeped with light, while garish vessels overflowed with gold-foil wrapped candy. Velvet swags with no obvious purpose hung from the ceiling. Great cascades of floral arrangements were suspended from gold-painted columns, set atop tables, and even attached to the walls. But the flowers were arranged haphazardly with no particular design or colour theme. Red roses were bunched with yellow daises, while lilac orchids were linked with blue carnations. The garishly decorated platform where Hadi and Munira would view, and be viewed by, the wedding guests was covered with blinking green and red lights!

I was so absorbed in this expensive but tasteless display that I did not see Sara come forward from the swarming throng.

A gentle arm went around my waist. 'Sultana.'

'Sara,' I smiled, 'thanks be to God you found me.'

With a disapproving look, Sara nodded at the scene around us. 'On this night I am embarrassed to be my brother's sister.'

'For more reasons than the décor, I too am ashamed,' I agreed.

'I wish I had helped you hide Munira,' Sara admitted.

'Truly?' I gasped.

'Yes. Our two hearts are as one on this issue.'

I embraced my sister and tried to comfort her as she comforted me.

'You were right not to encourage me, Sara. Ali would have sifted the very sands of the desert to find his daughter and hand her over to Hadi.' I sighed in sad resignation. 'There can be no escape for the daughter of such a man.'

Hand in hand, Sara and I began making our way through the room, greeting many aunts and cousins while we looked for our sisters.

Before the time arrived for Munira to make her appearance, all ten daughters of our beloved mother, Fadeela, had assembled in a circle.

But there was no joy among us. Each sister was greatly saddened by the reason for our reunion. Following Mother's death, Nura, the eldest daughter, had with our consent assumed the rank of leader of the sisters. She was the steadfast figure who often guided her younger sisters' paths by pointing out the reality of our lives. Stoic and strong, it would seem that Nura, of all the sisters, had attained mastery over her emotions. But on this evening, even Nura was subdued with sorrow. She had accompanied us to Egypt when Hadi's true character had become known by our family. Unlike many gathered there, she knew the corruption of the soul of the man who would soon possess Munira.

'This is a sad, sad night,' Nura muttered with her eyes fixed on the wedding dais.

Sara shuddered at the night she knew lay ahead of Munira. She sighed, 'If only the dear girl did not fear men so.'

'Whether she fears men, or loves men, this will be a cruel night,' Tahani said wearily.

I looked behind Tahani and saw that dear Reema, the fifth child of our mother, was discreetly manipulating the medical device that captured her body's waste. The device was well-hidden under her dress, but the anxious Reema had formed the habit of compulsively checking and rechecking the appliance. After her husband Saleem's brutal assault, Reema had needed a colostomy, and would never regain control over all her bodily functions.

Angry at that memory of yet another woman's suffering at the hands of a man, I asked hotly, 'How is it that we accept all this?'

'*Shhh*,' my sisters joined in unison to stop me from drawing the attention of the women standing close to us.

'It is my belief,' I said through clenched teeth, 'that we should be throwing stones at the

King's palace, rather than attending this shameful event.'

'Sultana,' Nura warned, 'do *not* create a scene.'

I even surprised myself with my impertinence. 'It is *you* who should be causing a scene with me, beloved sister.'

Nura did not reply, but she gave me a warning look.

'Every woman in Saudi Arabia should gather as many stones as she can carry,' I repeated, 'and throw them at our men.'

Eight of my nine sisters, Nura, Reema, Tahani, Baher, Dunia, Nayam, Haifa and Soha, gasped as one. Only Sara remained silent.

I watched them as they exchanged fretful expressions.

Seeing the disappointment etched on my face, and knowing that I was longing for a single brave act from all of them, Sara stepped forward and took my hand.

High-pitched trills suddenly erupted from behind closed doors. My sisters were saved from further trauma from me as the wedding procession began.

Trembling with anger and sorrow, I watched six beautiful dancers advance dramatically through the open doors. The women were trained dancers from Egypt, and were fitted out in elaborate costumes that displayed their voluptuous bodies. When the dancers passed our way, I was startled by their inviting winks.

I looked at Sara with a questioning eye, and she shrugged. I had heard that one of our female cousins had taken an Egyptian dancer as a lesbian lover, and wondered if the financial gain that dancer had enjoyed had put ideas into the heads of her associates.

Chanting female drummers, dressed in colourful embroidered dresses, followed the dancers. I recognized these women as Saudis from a tribe loyal to our family.

Twelve tiny girls between the ages of three and six followed the drummers. They were the flower girls, and were beautifully dressed in pink satin dresses with matching hair bows and shoes. They scattered petals plucked from purple orchids. From the fragrance that drifted towards me, I knew these petals to be specially scented with a sweet-smelling incense. These children were members of our royal family, and their endearing childish mannerisms brought many smiles from the watching crowd.

Once the dancers had circled the throne-like platform, they proceeded to dance themselves into a musical frenzy. This was the signal that the bride was making her way through the hall.

As a short woman, I needed to stand on my toes to improve my view.

Munira walked slowly down the lengthy hall. She was dressed in a soft-peach lace wedding dress. Her gloomy face was lightly covered by a sheer peach veil. Rhinestones sewn into the fabric of the veil reflected back off the room's lighting, achieving a dramatic twinkling effect that her eyes could not project. The heavy train of her dress was carried by young teenage cousins, who ranged in age from thirteen to nineteen. These girls were adorned in hideous orange satin costumes surely not of their choosing.

Overwhelmed by the swirl of misarranged colours

of flowers and costumes, I thought this to be the most unappealing wedding I had ever attended. Everything about this occasion was as mismatched as Hadi and Munira themselves, the bride and groom.

Sara and I exchanged incredulous looks. I knew that her thoughts were as mine.

When Munira walked past, I caught a glimpse of her pale face. Her eyes showed no expression, she looked straight ahead, an empty moment in time that seemed to last forever.

I felt wretched!

Once Munira was seated on the dais, the moment I so dreaded had finally arrived. The time had come for the arrival of the groom.

The loud voices in the room soon diminished to loud whispers.

Hadi, escorted by one of his brothers, walked towards the hapless Munira. Ali and a bearded *mutawwa* followed closely.

Munira was staring evenly at Hadi. A terrible pain flashed across her face, but the moment was fleeting. Knowing that she had been ensnared like an animal, and that there was no hope of release, Munira appeared courageously determined to maintain her dignity.

Hadi was not returning his bride's gaze, as would most grooms who are in view of the one they are to wed. Instead, he was looking hungrily at the uncovered faces of the female guests! Obviously the years had not changed him. He appeared to relish the rare opportunity to steal a long licentious look at unveiled women in an officially sanctioned setting. Had adulthood only reinforced the man's depraved nature?

Shocked at his salacious stares, the women responded in a low murmur of scandalized voices.

Sara clutched my arm so tightly that her fingers grew white. I knew she was afraid that I would pull from her grip, rush towards Hadi, and hit him with all the force I could gather.

It was hard to believe that things could get worse, but I had already made a quick decision that should Hadi give me a flirtatious look, I would spit in his face, then inform this crowd of royal ladies of all that I knew of this man.

The assemblage was saved from that exciting scene, for just as Hadi arrived at the place where we were standing, he tore his eyes away from the crowd and looked towards his neglected bride. A delighted smile crossed his face. He was indeed a fortunate man.

Nothing surprised me more than to observe that Hadi had barely aged from the time of our trip to Egypt so many years before! Surely one so evil should have degenerated into an ugly, wizened man? I had anticipated a corrupted appearance, but that was not the case. While Hadi had grown more stout, his face was still youthful. Who would guess that beneath Hadi's smooth skin lay the heart of a brute?

A bitter thought passed through my mind: our young girls are forced to sacrifice their youth so that men such as Hadi can feed on their beauty! It is by devouring young girls that such men remain robust. I was forced to hold back my tears.

Hadi joined Munira on the wedding platform, much pleased with himself.

I watched Ali as he made his way to the bridal pair's side, but then turned away. I mentally disassociated myself from him, my blood brother.

The official wedding ceremony had been conducted earlier in the week with the immediate families in attendance, although the bride and groom had not appeared in the other's presence. This occasion was for the purpose of celebration only.

Nura tried to force Sara and me to join our sisters in offering our good wishes to the bride and groom, but that we refused to do. How could we mimic gladness when one of the most immoral men we had ever known now claimed sole ownership of a sweet and innocent young woman of our own flesh and blood?

I smiled bitterly when I heard female cousins admire Munira's handsome and wealthy new husband. A silent prayer lingered unspoken on my tongue. Oh God, have mercy on Saudi women. And quickly!

My Secret

On the day following Munira's 'sanctified bondage', Kareem had to depart Saudi Arabia for a three-week business trip to Japan. Abdullah accompanied his father. The unhappy time had come for Abdullah to return to his university schooling in the United States, and the plan was for him to fly on to California after staying with Kareem for a few days in Japan. Tears came to my eyes each time I remembered that I would not see the handsome face of my beloved son for three long months.

Other than the servants, my daughters and I were alone in our palace in Riyadh. But these daughters were little comfort to their mother since they, too, were preparing for the coming school year. They preferred to spend the remaining time with their friends.

I have always been restless and easily bored, and I have to confess I am unceasingly inquisitive as to my children's activities. So I passed the empty hours by pacing up and down lonely hallways on the second floor of our home, pausing frequently at the doorways of my daughters' rooms. When they were younger, my daughters had shared the same wing. But now, because of Amani's determined penchant for destroying Maha's glossy fashion magazines and musical tapes, Kareem and I had moved Amani to a wing on the southside of the palace, while Maha remained in the north wing. Therefore, the steps I made were many.

My findings rarely varied. The sound of persistent chanting and praying usually drifted from within Amani's suite; while loud laughter and even louder American rock and roll music blared from behind Maha's door.

Bored with spying on my all-too-predictable daughters, I withdrew to my private quarters. With Munira's tragic plight exercising complete dominance over my mind, I was not in the mood to attend the usual women's afternoon parties at the homes of friends or relatives.

Hadi had taken his young bride to Morocco for a month-long honeymoon. Although I could barely bring myself to think of Munira's present agony, I did want confirmation that the poor child was all right. So, I telephoned Tammam to enquire if there was any news of the couple. I was incredulous when Tammam confessed that she had been too timid to ask Hadi for the telephone number of the hotel where the couple would be staying. I slammed down the telephone rather than risk a possible outburst at Tammam's maddeningly insipid behaviour.

There was nothing to do but to wait. To my dismay, I began to crave an alcoholic drink, although I fought my sinful desire.

A few hours later, a distraught Tammam called to report that Munira had surreptitiously telephoned while Hadi was out of their hotel room, to tell her mother that she detested and feared her new husband even more than she had ever believed possible.

Upon hanging up the telephone, sick with despair, I lay across the bed. A numbness spread over my body. How powerless I felt! There was nothing that I, or anyone else, could do to help Munira. She was legally wed to Hadi now.

Years before I had learned that no authority in our country would interfere with a private matter between a man and a woman. A thousand years would come and go, and the bodies of Saudi women would still be owned by Saudi men. How I hated our helplessness!

Tears flowed down my face. My heart was fluttering dangerously. I quickly determined to turn my mind to other matters. Yes, I would occupy myself with a task. I had been negligent in keeping an account of our family's stores of alcohol. I would make a surprise inspection. Not that I had any intention of having a drink, I promised myself, as I pulled a dressing gown over my head – I simply wanted to ensure that no-one was pilfering these costly and scarce supplies. Since alcoholic beverages are banned in Saudi Arabia, it is dauntingly expensive to acquire a large supply on the black market. One bottle of liquor costs anywhere from 200 Saudi riyals to 350 Saudi riyals ($55–$95).

I walked through our palace blind to the magnificence of our recently redecorated rooms that were rich in paintings, tapestries and antique European furniture. The year before, Kareem and I had employed a Milanese decorator, who had enthusiastically hired labourers to tear down walls, replace ceilings and windows, and build domed and vaulted rooms with lofty columns and concealed chambers. He had co-ordinated colours and textures, Persian carpets, silk drapes and marble floors and had added some pieces of Italian and French antique furniture. The combination of the arabesques and arches of Middle Eastern tradition with modern Italian flamboyance had resulted in a romantic informality that drew great envy and attention from my royal cousins.

I walked past the large sitting area into the cigar and wine athenaeum only to discover one of the Filipino servants at work dusting the redwood liquor cabinets. I abruptly told her to find another chore. When I was certain that she had left the room, I began to count the bottles. I was overjoyed to discover that Kareem had replenished our cache magnificently. There were over two hundred bottles of spirits as well as sixty bottles of assorted liqueurs.

With a light heart, I proceeded into the walk-in wine room, a spacious oak structure specially built to maintain proper temperature and humidity for our wine collection. At two hundred bottles, I stopped counting.

We were well-stocked, indeed, I thought. My mind then drifted into a dangerous arena. Surely Kareem would not notice the absence of a few bottles here and there. As I considered the plentiful supplies on hand, I was overcome with familiar cravings. My vow of abstinence was easily dismissed. I tucked two bottles of Scotch whisky under my loose gown, and pledging that I would allow myself only a single drink, I ascended the winding marble staircase to our private quarters.

Once inside, I locked the door and lovingly caressed the bottles I had seized. Then I began to drink, in the earnest hope that I might obliterate the image in my mind of Munira's on-going torment.

Twenty-four hours later I was jolted awake by the nearby sounds of hysterical voices. I opened my eyes when someone began to slap my face. I heard my name called out: 'Sultana!'

Sara's worried face hovered close to mine. 'Sultana! Can you hear me?'

I felt a pang of anxiety. Judging from my physical discomfort, I feared that I had been in an accident and was now awakening from a coma.

I heard Maha sobbing, 'Mother! Wake up!'

Sara comforted my daughter, 'Praise God, Maha! She is still with the living.'

Trying to shake off my confusion, I blinked my eyes. I wanted to speak, but I was unable to form words. I could hear the mingled languages of Filipino, Thai and Arabic being shouted by excited female voices. I wondered groggily why my bedroom was filled with so many chattering women!

In a weak voice, I asked my sister, 'What has happened?'

With furrows of pain lining her forehead, Sara seemed to search for words. 'Sultana,' she finally asked, 'how do you feel?'

'Not good,' I said, before repeating once again, 'What happened?'

The loud voice of Amani, rising in volume with every word, rang out over the rest. 'You have committed a grave sin, Mother!'

Choking back sobs, Maha shouted, 'Shut up! I mean it!'

Amani's words echoed through the room. 'I have the evidence, here!'

I turned my head and saw that Amani was enthusiastically swinging an empty whisky bottle in each hand. 'Mother has been *drinking*!' she shouted. 'Surely the Holy Prophet will curse her for this sin!'

Sara turned a sombre face to her niece. 'Amani, give me the bottles and then please leave the room.'

'But . . .'

Sara gently took the bottles from Amani's hands. 'Now, child. Do as I say. Leave the room.'

Next to her father, Amani loved and respected her Auntie Sara more than anyone. Now she obeyed, but not without a parting threat. 'I'm going to tell Father about this – the moment he arrives home.'

As dazed as I was, I could feel my stomach turn at the thought.

Sara carefully laid the empty bottles on the foot of my bed, and then she took charge: 'Everyone, leave the room.'

'Not me!' Maha wailed.

'Yes, you too, Maha.'

When Maha bent to kiss me, she whispered, 'Don't worry about Amani, Mother, I know how to quiet her foolish tongue.'

The expression in my eyes must have betrayed my curiosity, for Maha clarified, 'I'll threaten to tell all Amani's religious friends that she wears revealing clothes and flirts with boys!'

Even though this was not true, I knew that such a warning would cause Amani great concern, for her reputation is that of a true believer who could never commit a single sin. I knew this was wrong, but I also realized the graveness of my current situation should Kareem be alerted to my weakness. Therefore, I did not reprimand Maha, but I gave her a tight smile which she might take to signify reluctant approval.

As she left the room, Maha struggled to push the heavy wooden door against the door facings which I now noticed had been shattered.

Sara answered my unspoken question. 'When you would not respond to our cries, I ordered one of the drivers to knock down the door.'

Tears of humiliation came into my eyes.

'You lay like one dead, Sultana,' Sara said as she picked up a cloth and began to wipe my forehead. 'I feared the worst,' she said with a great sigh. She then took a glass of tomato juice and encouraged me to sip a little through a straw. 'Your silence frightened me out of my wits!' She plumped up the cushions under my head before sitting beside me on the bed.

Sara took a deep breath before saying, 'Sultana, you must tell me *everything* now.'

Although Sara appeared unperturbed, I could tell she was steeped in disappointment because it was reflected in her dark eyes. Feeling that death would be welcome for one as wretched as I, my shoulders shook as I began to weep in earnest.

Sara stroked my face and arms. Her voice was gentle as she told me a grim truth, 'Sultana, your daughters, and your servants, all tell me that you have begun drinking a great deal of alcohol.'

My eyes flew open. So, my furtive drinking had not been so secret after all!

Sara was waiting for an explanation. At that

moment, I knew that my sister could not understand the true source of my pain. I cried out, 'You still have little children who need you!'

I could tell by the bewildered grimace on Sara's face that she was beginning to fear for my mental, as well as my physical, well being.

Frustrated, I wailed, 'And you have your books!'

It was true! Sara had a great love for collecting books on a wide range of topics that interested her. Her life's hobby, collecting and reading books, gave her endless hours of joy and contentment. Sara's valuable library consisted of books in Turkish, Arabic, English, French and Italian. Her art books, stored in their special bookcases, were lovely beyond description. She had also amassed a priceless collection of ancient, handwritten manuscripts describing the golden age of the Arabs. I knew that if a great cataclysmic tragedy should ever leave Sara alone in the world, she would seek and find solace in her stacks of books.

'Sultana. What are you speaking about?'

'And your husband never leaves on long trips!' Asad's work rarely took him from his home, as did Kareem's. 'And Asad loves you more than Kareem loves me!'

Sara was married to Kareem's brother, Asad. I had known for many years that Kareem would never love me as intensely as Asad adored my sister. While I had never begrudged Sara Asad's great love, I often wistfully yearned for the same devotion from Kareem.

'Sultana!'

In between sobs of self-pity, I began to explain. 'My children are nearly grown – they no longer want their mother in their lives.' What I said was true. Abdullah had recently turned twenty-two, Maha was nineteen and Amani was seventeen. Three of Sara's six children were young enough that they still required their mother's daily attention.

'Sultana, please. You are not making sense.'

'Sara, nothing has turned out as I planned! None of my three children are dependent on me any longer . . . Kareem is away more than he is home . . . and there are countless abused women in the world like Munira crying out for help, and there's *nothing* that I can do to help them!' I began to sob hysterically. 'And now, I'm afraid I'm becoming an alcoholic.'

Facing the emptiness and humiliation of my life for the first time, I cried out, 'My life is a failure!'

Sara's arms wrapped around me in a warm embrace. 'Darling, you are the bravest person I've ever known. Shhh, little sister, now hush . . .'

Suddenly, Mother's image came to me. I wanted to be a child again, to be in those childhood places, to forget all of the adult disappointments in between. I wanted to go back in time. I shouted as loud as I could, 'I want Mother!'

'Shhh, Sultana. Please stop crying. Don't you know that Mother is around us, even now?'

My sobs began to soften as I looked around the room. I was longing to see Mother once again, even if her countenance only came to me in the form of an apparition, as before in my dreams. But I could see nothing, and said, 'Mother's not here.' After my sobs subsided, I described my dream to Sara. For me, the pain of our mother's death would never heal.

'You see,' Sara remarked, 'your dream proves

my words to be true. Mother's spirit is always with us. Sultana, I, too, often sense Mother's presence. She comes to me at the oddest moments. Only yesterday, when I was looking in a mirror, I clearly saw Mother appear behind me. I only caught a glimpse of her, but it was enough to let me know that the day will come when we will all be together once again.'

I felt a sense of peace wash over me. If Sara had also seen Mother, then I *knew* that Mother still existed. My sister's integrity is never questioned by anyone who knows her.

Sara and I sat quietly, both of us remembering the days when we were innocent children, and Mother's unending reservoir of wisdom, understanding and love sheltered us from most of life's dangers.

When I fidgeted under the bedcovers, the two empty whisky bottles dropped from the bed to the floor. Sara's haunted eyes looked towards the bottles, and then at me. Recalling the reason for the alarm that had brought Sara to my side, a black depression once again settled over me.

'You are on a dangerous path, Sultana,' Sara whispered.

I sat up and twirled my hair around my finger. After a time I burst out, 'I *hate* my life of idleness!'

'Sultana, you can do more with your life. You must take responsibility for your own happiness. A hobby or occupation that consumed your attention would be good for you.'

'How can I? The veil interferes with everything I do!' I grumbled. 'I can't believe that we were unlucky enough to be born in a country that forces its women to wear shrouds of black!'

'I thought it was loneliness that was driving you to drink,' Sara dryly noted. With eyes half-closed in weariness, she said, 'Sultana, I do believe that you would argue with Allah Himself!'

Filled with unruly emotions, unsure of the exact cause of my current turmoil, I looked at Sara and shrugged. 'Amani is right, you know. I have been cursed by the Prophet. And he must have cursed me on many occasions. Why else would everything bitter in my life come together at once?'

'You are being foolish, Sultana! I do not believe that our Holy Prophet would curse a troubled woman,' she said. 'Is it a life without problems that you are seeking?'

'*Inshallah*!' (God willing!)

'You want a life that does not exist, Little Sister. Everyone who lives has problems.' She paused, then said, 'Even kings suffer problems that cannot be resolved.'

I knew that she was referring to the failing health of our Uncle Fahd, the man who was the King of Saudi Arabia. As the years passed, he had become increasingly frail. He was now a man with everything in life but good health. When he had suffered a serious medical setback recently, every member of our family had been reminded of our own mortality, and the fact that all the money and modern health care in the world could not keep death at bay for ever.

Sara's firm tone relaxed. 'Sultana, you must learn to bear the pain of life without reaching for improper solutions.' She nudged a whisky bottle aside with her foot. 'You have become the slave of a new power, a power that is in danger of creating even more serious problems than the ones that drove you to drink!'

I then divulged my deepest fear. 'Amani might tell Kareem.'

Sara told me flatly, 'You tell him first. Anyhow, it's best not to keep secrets from your husband, Sultana.'

I looked closely at my sister. Without a trace of rancour, I realized that I had always been outshone by her beauty and by her virtue.

Even though she had been called from her home unexpectedly, Sara was impeccably dressed in a freshly ironed silk dress, with shoes of matching colour. An exquisite set of pearls were fastened around her delicate neck. Her thick black hair was fashioned in a flattering style; her skin lovely; her eyelashes were so long and thick that she required no make-up.

Sara's personal life paralleled her perfect appearance. Her marriage to Asad was the best I had ever known. I had never heard her raise her voice to her husband, or even complain about him. Many times I had tried to tempt Sara in to confiding a weakness belonging to her husband, without success. While I was guilty of shouting at, pinching and even slapping my children, I had never seen Sara lose control with any of her children. My sister was the satisfied mother of the six children that Huda, our family slave, had predicted so many years before.

Although problems occasionally arose with her second child, a daughter named Nashwa, Sara remained gently firm. She had even established a warm relationship with Asad and Kareem's mother, the unpopular and difficult Noorah. In addition, my sister was one of the few Al Sa'uds I knew who never drank alcohol or smoked cigarettes. Certainly, Sara had no secrets to keep from her husband. How could such a flawless woman ever understand that as I grew older, my bad habits had increased, rather than diminished?

It seemed that my life had always been imbued in some deep intrigue. My drinking was only one of the many secrets I kept from Kareem. Over the years of our marriage, I had presented myself in a more flattering light to my husband than was true. I even lied to Kareem about the number of kilos I had recently gained!

Not wishing to further disappoint my sister with additional knowledge of the weaker points of my character, I kept from blurting out everything that had come into my mind. Instead, I hastened to promise, 'I will never drink again, if only I do not have to confess to Kareem. I could not bear it. He would never forgive me.'

'Oh? What do you think Kareem might do?'

I stretched the truth mightily. 'Well, he might beat me.'

Sara's black eyes grew large with disbelief.

'You know yourself, Sara, that Kareem dislikes people who cannot control their habits. At the very least, his love for me will dim.'

Sara's hands fluttered. 'Then what will we do to destroy this habit? The servants told me that you drink to the point of drunkenness when Kareem is away.'

Indignantly I demanded, 'Who said such a thing?'

'Sultana. Curb your anger. The information was given out of genuine concern for your well-being.'

'But . . .'

Sara's voice was firm and unsympathetic. 'No. I will not tell you.'

I tried to think which of the servants might have spied on me, but with so many women in the palace, there was no way to be certain where to direct my anger.

Sara pursed her lips, thinking. 'Sultana, I have an idea. Ramadan will soon be upon us. At that time, you will be unable to eat or drink during the daylight hours anyway. And, when Kareem is not with you, we can make sure Maha or I remain by your side. That will be the time to defeat this sinful craving.' Sara leaned towards me with a smile. 'We will spend much time together.' I heard the warm affection in her voice. 'It will be like our days together when we were children!'

I began to chew my fingernails, remembering the one major problem that still remained. 'But how will we prevent Amani from telling Kareem?'

Sara pulled my hand from my mouth and held it between her two hands. 'I will speak with her, don't worry.'

I was a prisoner reprieved! I knew that if Maha's threat did not frighten Amani into silence, then Sara would surely manage to convince my child not to speak to Kareem. I smiled happily, knowing that under Sara's watchful eye, all would be well. Slowly, my worries began to lift.

Finally able to relax, I asked, 'I'm feeling hungry now. Can you stay for a meal?'

Sara nodded slightly. 'I'll call home to say that I will be staying a while longer.'

I rang the kitchen on the palace intercom and asked the head cook what had been prepared for the midday meal. Pleased with what I heard, I expressed my approval. I then instructed her that my sister and I would eat our meal in the garden since cloudy skies had led to weather that was cooler than usual.

After I washed my face and hands and slipped on a fresh dress, Sara and I made our way through the palace to the outside gardens. We walked arm-in-arm under a row of leafy trees that provided a cool shade along the passageway. We paused to admire the flowering bushes now heavy with red and gold blossoms.

With our unlimited Al Sa'ud wealth, we can do many wonderful things, even turn a parched desert into a green garden!

The food had not yet arrived, but we settled into the comfortable chairs surrounding the glass-top table. A red awning shaded the area around the table.

Soon three Filipino servants appeared balancing silver trays heavy with dishes. While waiting to be served, Sara and I sipped hot, sugary tea and discussed the school plans of our children. Once the servants set the table and filled our plates, we talked and laughed while we ate our way through a feast of salads, meatballs cooked in sour cream and roast chicken stuffed with boiled eggs and rice.

I remembered Sara's words about the approach of Ramadan. With that thought in mind, I took second servings of many dishes, knowing that during Ramadan I would have to endeavour to abstain from food between the daylight hours.

As I savoured the food before me, my thoughts drifted to what lay ahead for me during this time of sacrifice. Muslims throughout the world would soon begin to search the skies for the new moon. Once that sighting occurred, the time for fasting would have arrived.

My burning desire was that, for the first time in my life, I would be able to fulfil my Muslim oath.

Chaining the Devil

Ramadan is one of the five pillars of Islam and it is obligatory that every adult Muslim observe its customs. The Koran says: 'O ye who believe! Fasting is prescribed to you as it was prescribed to those before you that you may (learn) self-restraint and remain conscious of God . . .' (2:183)

Although I breathe somewhat easier during this special month, knowing that the doors of heaven are open and the doors of hell are closed, with the devil chained and unable to create mischief, a strict dedication to Ramadan has never suited my particular character.

I've always been possessed with a great longing to be as pious as my mother and sisters, but I must admit that I have not been flawless in my devotions. Even as a child, when I first learned of the rituals of Ramadan, I knew that my failure to conform was inevitable. For instance, I was told to impose silence on my tongue and avoid lying, obscene language, laughing and backbiting. My ears were to be closed to anything offensive. My hands should not reach out for evil; as my feet should be curbed from pursuing wickedness. If I inadvertently allowed heavy dust or thick smoke to enter my throat, my fast would be considered invalid! Not only was I not to eat or drink during the hours between dawn and sundown, but, even when rinsing my mouth, I was warned to guard against accidentally swallowing a single drop of water. Most important of all, I was to fast from my heart, meaning that all worldly concerns should be discarded, and only thoughts of Allah should enter my mind. Lastly, I must atone for any thought or action that might distract me from remembering Allah.

From the time I began fasting at adolescence, I was often forced to atone for my failure to achieve full compliance. The Koran says that, 'Allah will not take you to task for that which is unintentional in your oaths, but He will take you to task for the oaths which you swear in earnest. The expiation therefore is the feeding of ten of the needy with the average of that you feed your own, or the clothing of them, or the liberation of a slave . . .' (5:89)

Since the time of our marriage, Kareem and I had lost count of the number of needy persons that my failure to keep my Ramadan vows had fed and clothed.

As I savoured my second serving of honeyed dessert, I silently vowed that, this year, I would astonish my family with my faithful adherence to Ramadan.

After Sara left to return to her own palace, I busied myself devoutly studying the Koran, in an effort for the spiritual month ahead.

Ten nights later an enthusiastic announcement resonated from the neighbourhood mosque informing believers that the holy month of Ramadan was upon us. The new moon had been first sighted by a group of trustworthy Muslims in a small Egyptian village. I knew that the same happy message was being heard at every corner of the world where Muslims reside. The time had come for all Muslims to strive to move towards a state of perfection.

We were six days into Ramadan when Kareem returned to Riyadh to join his family in keeping the important rituals.

When Amani assured her Auntie Sara that she would not reveal my drinking to Kareem, I made a vow that never again would I supply my God-fearing daughter with such a noose to dangle before my eyes.

I felt a glimmer of hope that all would now be well.

During the month of Ramadan, every routine of our normal life is altered. We rise at least an hour before dawn. Ablutions are made, verses of the Koran recited and prayers performed. Then a pre-dawn meal, called *sahoor* – usually consisting of cheese, eggs, yogurt or milk, fresh fruit and bread – is placed before us. We have to take care to finish this meal before the white thread of dawn appears, distinct from the black of night. After eating, but before the actual rising of the sun, more dawn prayers are performed.

For the remainder of the day, we are required to abstain from food, drink, smoking and sexual intercourse. During the day, we pray at noon and again in the late afternoon.

As soon as the sun retreats from the sky, our fast is broken by drinking a small amount of water, juice or milk. At this time, a prayer is offered: 'O God! I have fasted for Your pleasure. O God! Accept my fast and reward me.' Only then can we take nourishment. The usual food that breaks our fast is dates. After this light snack, the time quickly arrives for the sunset prayer and the dinner meal.

Each day before the sun sets during the month of Ramadan, the members of our extended families usually meet at the palace of Sara and Asad to socialize and to share the evening's banquet. A mood of celebration is always in the air, for our dispositions are generally improved due to the success of our self-control.

This celebratory atmosphere increases as the month of Ramadan draws to a close. Muslims begin to prepare for Eid ul-Fitr, the three-day feast which marks the close of Ramadan. While many devout Muslims prefer the austere period of striving for perfection, I find the celebration of Eid the most pleasurable time.

Since I have no particular schedule during the month of Ramadan, I usually turn my night into day and stay awake throughout the night. I watch videotapes of American films, read the Koran or play Solitaire. Once Kareem leaves our home for his office, I sleep late into the day, resting through the hours that bring me the greatest hunger and thirst so that I will not be tempted to break my fast. I do always take great care to rise from bed for my noon prayer, and then again for the mid-afternoon prayer, often offering extra supplications at this time.

During this particular Ramadan Sara often shared these difficult hours with me as she had promised. When Sara could not leave her own family, Maha stayed resolutely by my side. Although I was often listless and hungry during the afternoon hours, I knew that soon it would be the hour of sundown, when Kareem would return home to take us to Sara's palace.

By the nineteenth day of the Ramadan fast, I had not broken a single vow! I felt increasingly proud that I had not once been tempted to sneak a bit of food, drink a sip of water or smoke even one cigarette! Most importantly, I had successfully conquered my temptation to drink alcohol.

Kareem and Maha offered me many encouraging smiles and compliments. Sara congratulated me at every opportunity. Even Amani showed more warmth towards me. Never had I gone so long into Ramadan without sliding down that slippery slope of uncontrolled desires.

I honestly believe that, for once, I would have accomplished the total perfection I was so eagerly seeking, were it not for my hated brother, Ali. Although he knew his sisters' feelings about Munira's marriage, Ali still insisted that Hadi and his new bride join our extended family at the nineteenth sundown breaking of our fast. The couple had returned from their honeymoon in Morocco on the previous evening.

But Hadi was not a man welcome in our inner circle, and we had assumed that he and his four wives and children would be joining his own family when breaking the daily fasts. So when Sara informed me that Hadi and Munira would be among her guests, I guessed that we would be forced to witness poor Munira's first public subjugation. Furious at the thought, I spat, 'How can we be joyous with such a one as Hadi at our table?'

'This will be a difficult evening,' Sara agreed as she rubbed my back. 'But, we must get through it with good grace.'

The clenching of my jaw muscles hardened my voice. 'Hadi married Munira for one thing only! He's always wanted the opportunity to insinuate himself into the family life of the royals!'

Helplessly, Sara raised her hands into the air. 'There is nothing that we can do, Sultana. He is married to our brother's child. Anything we do to anger Hadi will come down on Munira's head.'

'It's the same as blackmail,' I muttered angrily.

Maha whispered into Nashwa's ear, and both girls laughed loudly.

Sara and I stared at our daughters.

My voice grew loud with increasing irritation. 'Why do you laugh?'

Maha's face reddened, and even before she spoke, I could tell that she was weaving a small lie. 'We were talking about a girl at school, Mother. Nothing more.'

'Daughter! Do not break your fast with a lie! Have you forgotten that it is Ramadan?'

'Nashwa?' Sara's voice was gentle.

Nashwa was a girl resembling Maha in many ways, but she had greater difficulty lying to her mother than my child did.

'It was only a small joke, Mother.'

'And? Share the joke, please.'

Nashwa exchanged an uneasy look with Maha, then said, 'Well, Maha wants us to cast a spell on Hadi so that his male organ will enter a permanent sleep.'

'Child!' Sara was aghast. 'Put such thoughts out of your mind! Only Allah has such power!'

I was angry that Maha could lie so easily, while Nashwa could not. I looked suspiciously at my daughter. Was Maha still drawn to the trickery of black magic?

Maha began to squirm under my scrutiny. Four or five years earlier, she had been caught planning to cast an evil spell on her own brother. But I thought that Kareem and I had frightened her into giving up all thoughts of black magic. Perhaps not, I now mused. I knew that a number of my royal relatives had a great belief in the black arts.

I did not share my thoughts with Sara, but secretly I agreed that Munira's life would take a turn for the better if her husband became impotent. After all, she could successfully appeal for divorce should such a thing occur. In Saudi Arabia a man can divorce his wife at any time without stating a cause, while Saudi women are not so fortunate. However, if a husband is impotent, or does not provide for his family, a divorce, however difficult, is possible for a woman to obtain.

Later, when Hadi and Munira arrived, the first thing I saw was the misery on Munira's face. I was so shocked at her wretched physical condition, I wanted to strike Hadi with all my force. In only one short month Munira had lost many kilos in weight, and now her skeletal frame was visible through her flesh.

Sara and I exchanged a horrified look.

Sara rose to her feet. 'Munira, you look unwell, child. Come and sit.'

Munira looked to Hadi for his approval.

Already the spirit of life has been sapped from her body!

Hadi moved his head slightly and made a clicking

noise with his tongue that meant no.

Obediently, Munira remained by her husband's side.

Hadi snapped his fingers and signalled at Munira. 'Coffee.'

Although the palace had many servants ready to satisfy our every whim, Hadi wanted to show us that one of our own was enslaved by him!

Understanding that the women of her family were aghast at her predicament, Munira's face grew red with shame as she stared at the floor.

'Munira!' Hadi said, loudly. An ugly scowl crossed his face.

Munira stumbled towards the kitchen, looking for coffee.

Hadi's scowl melted into a gloat. He turned to look at Munira's family. The satisfaction on his face was unbearable to see!

Sara stood and stared, looking at Nura, then to Hadi and back. She did not know what to do in the face of Hadi's intentional rudeness to his young wife. Other than poor Reema, all the daughters of Fadeela had respectful husbands, and even Saleem did not denigrate Reema in full view of her family.

Just as Munira returned from the kitchen carrying Hadi's coffee, Ali arrived.

My brother has always had the power to provoke me. Now, like the snake he is, Ali slithered his massive body up to Hadi and had the nerve to ask him if his honeymoon exercises had kept him so occupied that he had failed to enjoy the sultry beauty of the Moroccan women.

Munira's face flushed a deep crimson red, humiliated by her father's salacious comments.

I began to shake with rage. Did Ali not remember that his daughter was a shy girl who wanted nothing in life but to be left alone?

Suddenly, I could take no more. My brother was an unfeeling mass of human flesh who did not deserve to live! I jumped to my feet with violence on my mind.

Kareem had been watching, and when he recognized the reckless mood that had overtaken me he rushed to my side. Taking me by the arm, he forcibly led me towards another corner of the large room. Sara and Nura quickly joined us.

Ali looked mystified when he caught me casting him a murderous look. Not only was he compassionless, I decided, he was also simple-minded! He truly had no understanding that his every word wounded his innocent daughter. For Ali, women were a man's property, possessions whose feelings and well-being never need enter his realm of thinking.

My sisters and Kareem encouraged me to go to Sara's quarters and rest for a short while. They had witnessed many altercations between Ali and me, and hoped to avoid a disorderly scene that would surely disrupt the night's banquet.

I said that I thought that Sara and Asad should order Ali and Hadi out of their home.

Nura swallowed once or twice and looked to Sara. 'We are in your home, Sara. Do as you like.'

'We must think of Munira,' Sara reminded us all in her soothing voice. 'Anything we do to anger Hadi will be detrimental to her.'

I voiced my objection forcefully. 'How could it be worse? She is the slave of a man who loves nothing more than to torture women! At least if we attack him, then he will know that his behaviour does not meet with the approval of his wife's family!'

Without responding, Sara and Kareem led me away, while Nura rejoined the rest of the family. I could hear Ali and Hadi laughing and joking even as we left the room.

After convincing me that a short nap would restore calm thinking, Kareem and Sara left me alone. But the mental picture of Munira's shame kept sleep from coming. I fretfully thrashed from side to side, brooding over the never-ending abuse of females born in my country. We Saudi women owned nothing but our souls, and only because no man had yet devised a method to seize them!

Just as I was about to close my eyes, I spotted a bottle of wine sitting on a small table in the corner of the room. Although Sara did not drink, her husband Asad was a connoisseur of fine French wines.

I reasoned that I needed a drink rather than a nap. Nothing would quell my emotions better than a full-flavoured glass of French wine. For many days now, since the day Sara had rescued me from my drunken haze, I had not consumed a single drink. I counted the days and nights in my mind. For the past twenty-nine days and nights, I had been more self-controlled than I ever dreamed that I could be.

Now, abandoning every thought of Ramadan, as well as my promise to my sister, I threw back the bedcovers and moved towards that bottle as one bewitched. It was nearly full, and I happily grabbed it tightly. I then searched for a cigarette. Although I am a heavy smoker, I had not smoked a cigarette since the hour before dawn. I glanced at Asad's bedside clock. It was at least another hour before the breaking of the fast, but I knew that I could not wait that long. Unable to find what my body was craving, I slipped from Sara's bedroom and went across the hall into Asad's quarters. Surely cigarettes could be found there.

Several packets of Rothmans, a familiar but foreign brand of cigarettes, were strewn around Asad's bedroom. A gold cigarette lighter lay on his bedside stand. Now that I had my hoard, I knew it would be best to find a secluded spot to have a drink and a cigarette. Sara's bedroom would not do. Kareem or Sara might go there to assure themselves that I was indeed resting. I made a quick decision to hide in Asad's bathroom.

I had never seen my brother-in-law's bathroom, but I was not surprised at its large size. I lifted a glass from the bathroom sink before sitting down on an elaborate velvet bench.

With trembling hands, I lit my first cigarette of the day. After drawing the pleasing fumes into my lungs, I removed the silver stopper from the wine bottle and filled the glass. Alternately, I sipped Asad's wine and enjoyed his cigarette. For a small moment, life was good once again.

Just as I was savouring my secret treasures, I heard the sound of approaching footsteps. The terror of being discovered surged through my body like an electric shock. Quickly, I ran into Asad's large shower and closed the glass door.

Too late, I realized that I had left the open wine bottle on the floor beside the bench! My cigarette still burned, so I crushed it on the side of the shower tile and attempted to blow the cigarette smoke away.

The door creaked slightly as it opened. The large form of a man cast a shadow on the shower door as he sauntered into the room.

Luckily the glass door of Asad's shower was engraved with large black swans. I peered around the swans. The intruder was my brother, Ali!

I might have known.

Although I could not see details clearly, I closed my eyes when my brother lifted his *thobe*, lowered his undershorts, and began to urinate. Repulsed by the noise of his water, I placed my fingers in my ears. He urinated so long that I began to realize that such an amount could not be passed from one who had been fasting from liquids for an entire day. I knew then that Ali took the vows of Ramadan less seriously than he would want others to know. That knowledge pleased me mightily, and I could barely stifle my laughter at the thought of Ali's likely reaction should I jump from the shower and confront him.

After flushing the toilet and arranging his clothes, Ali stood for a few moments before the large wall mirror. He patted his cheeks, ran his fingers over his thick moustache and eyebrows, and smacked his large lips several times as he admired his mirrored reflection.

I was barely able to contain my amusement. I had to hold my hands over my mouth to keep from bursting into laughter.

As Ali turned to leave the room, the bottle of wine caught his eye. He stared thoughtfully at the bottle for a short moment, then walked rapidly towards it and drank the entire contents.

He peered at the label. 'Ah. A good year,' he commented to himself, before dropping the empty bottle in a wastebasket and leaving the room.

I slumped against the wall. I had wanted that wine! Then I began to giggle at the absurdity of it all, but, after wiping the tears of merriment from my face, I was struck by a disagreeable thought. When it came to abstinence, Ali and I were as one in our failure and hypocrisy. I could no more chain the devil in my soul than Ali could!

I returned to our family gathering in a subdued mood. With a new humility, I found myself more tolerant of Ali than I could have imagined earlier in the evening.

Poor Munira did not speak a single word during the course of the long meal. She sat silently by her husband's side while nibbling at a small mound of chicken and rice.

My sisters and I exchanged many worried glances during that evening. Our hearts turned over more than once, yet we had no power to change the stream of Munira's life. Each of us feared that life for Munira could be little more than an accumulation of great sufferings. We were helpless. Only Allah could save Munira.

Paradise Palace

Since the time I was a young girl, I have always believed that dreams once dreamed are never truly lost. And so, despite the discouraging truth that on the nineteenth day of Ramadan I broke my fast by smoking a cigarette, and, most blasphemous of all, by drinking a forbidden glass of wine, I still dreamed of becoming a saintly Muslim on the same exalted level as my mother and my sisters. I hoped I might still become a righteous person, despite my lapses. I resolved that there was no need to add humiliation to discomfort by confessing failure to members of my family. In any event, I had little doubt that God had witnessed my sinful behaviour, and to me that alone was shame enough. My only hope was that Mother had been so occupied with her own spiritual life that her daughter's dishonourable conduct on earth had gone unnoticed.

Kareem was another matter. The day before Ramadan ended, we travelled to our palace located in Jeddah on the Red Sea. In the late afternoon, I was sitting in the garden with Kareem and my daughters while waiting for the last day of Ramadan to end. I noticed that Kareem was watching me carefully. He looked so thoughtful that I began to feel anxious. Had Amani failed to keep her promise to Sara? Had my daughter told Kareem about my disgraceful and intoxicated condition while he was in Japan?

I wanted to ask Kareem what was on his mind, but I feared the subject of his introspection might be something I did not want to discuss. When Kareem began to speak, I cringed.

'Sultana,' he said with a smile, 'I want you to know that I am very proud of you.'

Anticipating criticism, I was confused by this compliment. I sat and stared without speaking. What was his intent?

He repeated, 'Yes. I am very proud.' Kareem looked at me with such affection that I thought he might kiss me. But since this conversation was taking place during the daylight hours, and we were still in our Ramadan fast, he merely stroked my hands.

Bewildered, I could only sputter, 'Proud?'

'Yes, my darling.' Kareem's smile widened. 'Sultana, since the first year we wed, I have witnessed the great struggle you undergo each Ramadan. I know that for you to succeed in your fast is a thousand times more remarkable than it is for an ordinary person.'

I squirmed, uncertain what I should do. While I had determined it best not to confess my failure to keep my fast, I felt overwhelmed with guilt at accepting congratulations for a feat I had not accomplished. The weight of my conscience came down full force on my heart.

I knew that I must tell my husband the truth, no

matter how disagreeable it might be for both of us. 'But, Kareem—'

'Do not protest, Sultana. You should be, and you will be, greatly rewarded for fulfilling your vows.'

'Kareem, I . . .'

'Darling, I realized long ago that Allah creates some people to be more highly spirited than others. And I believe that He does this for a great purpose. Although such people can create turmoil, often it is for the best.' He smiled sweetly as he stared into my face. 'You are just such a person, Sultana.'

'No, no, Kareem, I need to tell you that—'

Kareem put his finger across my lips. 'I've often thought that you feel more deeply than anyone I've ever known, and that your profound feelings often bring you great suffering.'

'*Kareem, listen . . .*'

Maha interrupted. 'Father is right, Mother. You will be rewarded many times over for conquering your desire for earthly pleasures.' Maha turned a cheerful look at Kareem. 'I'm very proud of Mother, also.'

I shouted, 'No! You do not understand!' I placed my head in my hands and let out a low cry. 'You do not understand! I must make atonement!'

At that moment, I finally felt that I had the courage to explain the reasons for my desperate need to make amends, and to confess that I was less pure than either of them believed.

But Amani chose that same moment to taunt me, sneering, 'You praise a Muslim for doing what is the minimum normal requirement for every Muslim?'

Ignoring Amani, Kareem's tone was puzzled as he pulled my hands away from my face. 'Atonement? For what, Sultana?'

I realized I was unwilling to confess my shortcomings in front of such an unforgiving child as Amani. I let out a deep breath. 'I must make additional reparations for past sins.'

I felt guilty seeing Kareem's eyes glisten in pride and affection. How could I sink so low? Lowering my head, I mumbled, 'I've always been so sinful, as you know.'

Now I was being manipulative, even more reason for guilt! I was certain that God would severely punish me for continuing such shameless deception. I made a silent but sincere vow that I would wait no longer than until the first moment Kareem and I were alone to right this wrong. I would confess everything.

My thoughts drifted to Mother. I sighed and unintentionally spoke aloud, 'I wish Mother was with us.'

Amani spitefully declared, 'Only the weak cannot accept the will of God.'

I stared at Amani with a long look of resigned misery.

She opened her mouth as though to insult me once again, but Kareem gave her a stern and reproachful glare. 'We are practically at the end of Ramadan, Amani, and you insult your mother?'

This stopped Amani from saying more.

Suddenly, a melodious voice came over the neighbourhood mosque loudspeaker announcing that the new moon for the month of *shawwal*, which is the tenth *hijra* month, had been sighted and confirmed. Ramadan was over! The celebration of Eid-ul-Fitr could now begin. We expressed our joy by embracing and congratulating each other and our servants, each of us asking God to keep us in good health until the next Ramadan.

My favourite time of Ramadan had arrived, although my joy was somewhat tempered by the knowledge that I had not yet made atonement.

Eid, the most special holiday of Islam, continues for three days and is marked by a variety of events organized by the government, including fireworks, poetry recitals, dramas, painting contests and folk-singing concerts. Individuals celebrate by visiting family and friends, and bringing gifts.

We celebrated into the night until the golden rays of morning sunlight began to appear on the horizon. Thus, there was no opportunity that night to confess to Kareem.

The next morning, we did not wake from our exhausted sleep until noon. As I lay in bed, I steeled myself to tell Kareem of my broken oaths, but as soon as he finished dressing, he reminded me that he would be spending much of the day at the Jeddah palace of our beloved King Fahd. Kareem's mind was already so engrossed with the various traditions of Eid, that I thought it best that I leave our talk until later.

Still, I found myself in a quandary. Whether or not I confessed to Kareem, I still must make appropriate reparations. And I must do so before I started my round of visitations and gift-giving.

Just as Kareem was about to walk out the door, I ran towards him and took him by the arm. 'Darling, did you forget? I feel a great desire to feed many poor people this year.' My fingers plucked at his sleeve. 'Even more than in previous years.'

Kareem smiled. 'Do I need to feed more poor families than I did when you ate that large plate of *maamool bel tamur*?' (Pastries filled with dates.)

I reddened as I bit down on my lip. 'Yes.'

That humiliating incident had happened two years before during Ramadan. Our cooks had spent many hours mixing the spices, flour and dates for the pastry that our family would enjoy after the evening meal. All through the morning, the scent of that delicious pastry had drifted throughout the palace, causing me to salivate with longing for my favourite dessert. I was so hungry from fasting that I lost all good sense, and fantasized about date pastries all day.

Later that afternoon, once I knew that everyone was resting in their rooms, I slipped into the kitchen. I was so focused on the thought of tasting those pastries that I did not notice Kareem. Using the refrigerator door to shield myself from view, I consumed one pastry after another.

Kareem watched silently as I continued my voracious eating. Later he told me that once he saw the first pastry disappear into my mouth, he pragmatically decided that I might as well satisfy my hunger, as the sin of eating many pastries was the same as that of eating one.

Kareem's mischievous smile grew wider as he watched me squirm at that memory. 'Surely, Sultana, there is no need to feed as many families as I did last year when you smoked more than a packet of cigarettes during Ramadan. Is there?'

'Stop, Kareem!' I turned around angrily. 'Do not tease me!'

But Kareem continued. 'Yes, I discovered you crouching inside one of your closets, surrounded by discarded cigarette butts.'

He laughed gently at the memory, mingling tenderness with his teasing. 'Come, tell me, Sultana, what sin is it that you have committed this time?'

God finally had given me the opening that I had been praying for, but I had already decided there wasn't time to make my confession this morning.

'I've done nothing!' I declared defensively. 'I simply want to share our great wealth with those less fortunate.'

Kareem looked at me sceptically.

'Is not our good fortune an obligation for generosity?' I asked.

In his rush to join his cousins and uncles at the palace of the king, Kareem took me at my word. 'All right, Sultana. I'll have Mohammed purchase enough food to feed thirty needy families. Is that enough to cover your sins?'

'And tell Mohammed to buy them clothing, also,' I quickly added.

Mohammed was a loyal Egyptian employee. He would not gossip to the other servants about the large atonement that our family was making.

'And clothing, too.' Kareem agreed wearily.

I breathed a sigh of relief. As whoever breaks an oath becomes liable for the penalty of feeding ten needy persons, I thought that feeding and clothing thirty families would be more than sufficient to cover my sin of breaking the fast and drinking wine.

After Kareem left our quarters, I called out for Libby, one of my Filipino female servants, to prepare my bath. I felt lighthearted and free to have my sins so easily reconciled by mere almsgiving, and I began to sing Arabic love ballads as I soaked in my bath.

Once I had adorned myself with make-up and perfume, my Egyptian hairdresser arranged my long black hair in a complicated fashion consisting of braids, which she fastened in place with expensive hair clasps that I had recently bought at Harrods in London. Searching through the many dresses in my closet, I selected one of my favourite red satin gowns designed by Christian Dior.

Once I was satisfied with my reflection in the mirror, I called out whether Maha and Amani were ready, because I was eager to begin an afternoon of celebrating the Eid festival by visiting various relatives.

I watched attentively as three of the servants loaded the many gifts my daughters and I would present to our family and friends into the trunk of our new Mercedes. The elegantly wrapped gift boxes contained delicate chocolates moulded in the form of a mosque, silk scarves embroidered with golden threads, bottles of the finest French perfumes, colognes and pearl necklaces.

I knew exactly the palace that I wanted to visit first! The previous year an eccentric cousin whom we didn't know very well had built a magnificent palace that I had long been anxious to visit, because I had heard many fantastic stories of its wonders from friends. This cousin, named Faddel, had reportedly spent unimaginable sums of money to construct a palace and surrounding gardens to closely resemble the likeness of paradise itself – the heavenly paradise as described in our Holy Koran.

The Holy Koran gives many details of the glory

and pleasure that await those who honour God by living the earthly life of a good Muslim. Patient and obedient souls can look forward to spending eternity in one vast garden, watered with pleasant streams and shaded with trees. Dressed in silk and jewels, they will spend their time reclining on couches while eating the finest food. Wine will not be forbidden, as it is on earth, but will be served in silver goblets carried by handsome servants.

For a Muslim man fortunate enough to reach paradise, yet another reward awaits him. Seductively beautiful virgins, not yet touched by another man, will attend to his every need, and fulfil his every sexual desire. Each man will possess seventy-two of these lovely virgins.

Pious women will also enter paradise, and it is said that these women will receive the greatest joy from reciting the Koran and experiencing the supreme ecstasy of beholding Allah's face. All around these women will be children who never grow old. Of course, since Muslim women do not have any sexual desires, there will be no sexual partners awaiting them in paradise.

Although I was filled with the greatest curiosity, wondering how my cousin Faddel had emulated the wonders of paradise on earth, I also had a feeling of foreboding. For some reason, my heart was telling me not to go to that palace, to turn back. Despite this warning, I plunged ahead, taking along my two daughters.

Upon our arrival at 'Paradise Palace', as one of our cousins had mockingly named it, our driver found the iron gate to the entrance locked. The gate guard was nowhere to be seen. Our driver went to search for him, and reported that he could see two bare feet protruding from under the guard's chair through the gatehouse window.

I ordered our driver to pound on the glass partition. Finally, a sleepy Yemeni guard awoke and opened the gate, and at last, we were able to enter.

Although the driveway was made of many costly polished stones reflecting a glittering lustre, it provided a jolting ride for those arriving in a car. I looked about with great interest as we passed under the dense branches of a thicket of trees. Once we had passed through the grove of trees, we saw before us a scene of breathtaking beauty.

Faddel's palace was not one large building, as I had expected, but rather a succession of snowy-white pavilions. Perhaps as many as fifteen or twenty identical pavilions with billowing sky blue roofs were arranged in a circle around a larger pavilion, creating an imposing sight.

The grass surrounding the pavilions provided a lush carpet of green. Colourful beds of rare flowers were artfully arranged throughout the grounds. The combined colours of the white pavilions, the blue-tented roofs, the green grass and vivid blossoms were truly an inspired and beautiful composition.

'Look, children,' I said, 'the grass here is as green as my new emerald necklace!'

Maha exclaimed, 'There are more than ten pavilions!'

'Eighteen,' Amani said in a flat tone of voice.

'Amani,' I said, pointing at an ornate gold sign with 'Stallions' written on it in green lettering. 'There's a path leading to the stables.'

I was somewhat surprised that the Faddel I

knew had stables. While a large number of my cousins purchase and breed expensive horses, I had never heard of Faddel having an interest in horses.

Amani leaned over me to peer at that sign, but said nothing.

Our driver followed a winding road that took us beneath an imposing white marble arch. This surely was the entrance to the largest pavilion. A tall, handsome Egyptian doorman opened the door of our Mercedes and welcomed us profusely, then rushed forward to open the immense double doors that led into a large reception room. The doorman stood thus, waiting while our driver retrieved the gifts I had selected for this cousin and his wife.

Once satisfied that I had the appropriate packages in hand, I moved into the reception room. My daughters followed along behind me. We were greeted in perfect Arabic by a lovely young Asian woman who introduced herself as Layla. She smiled sweetly as she welcomed us as the first guests of the day. She reported that her mistress, our cousin Khalidah, would be with us shortly. Meanwhile, she would escort us to the main residence.

As I followed Layla, I carefully took note of everything that dazzled my eyes, as none of my sisters, nor even Kareem, had visited this so-called 'Paradise Palace'.

We were led down a wide corridor. The walls were covered in pale yellow silk with a delicate floral design. The carpet featured many lively patterns of exotic flowers and wildly colourful birds. It sank under our feet as we walked.

Amani suddenly asked Layla, 'Where do you keep the birds that I hear?'

Only then was I aware of a distant chorus of birds.

Layla laughed lightly. 'What you hear is only a recording.' Her voice sounded as pleasant and musical as the melody of the birds. 'The master insists that every sound heard here be pleasing to the ear.'

'Oh,' Amani replied.

Master? I thought to myself. Cousin Faddel?

Maha began to question the young woman who was near to her own age. We learned that Layla had been working in Saudi Arabia for Faddel and his wife, Khalidah, for the past five years. She proudly added that with her wages she was very happy to be able to support her large family who lived in Colombo, the capital city of Sri Lanka.

Amani was abrupt with the question that I hesitated to ask. 'Why do you have an Arabic name, Layla?'

The young woman smiled once again. 'I am not a Hindu. I am a Muslim. My family descended from Arab seafarers.' She paused before saying, 'Of course, only Muslims are allowed to enter this paradise.'

Maha nudged me with her elbow, but I managed to keep my face composed.

The long corridor suddenly opened up into an immense round room. Ornamental columns, lavish furniture, crystal chandeliers and clocks, priceless tapestries, vast mirrors and elegant ceramic panels came together in a stunning overall effect.

Several low divans covered in soft-coloured silks were neatly aligned under arched windows composed of intricate triangles of jewel-toned stained glass that depicted scenes of famous Arab warriors in battle. Sparkling clear water flowed from a two-tiered, silver-edged fountain. Chinese porcelain vases were centred on tables of polished mahogany inset with mother-of-pearl designs. A blue-tile floor glistened underneath the edges of the thick Persian carpets.

Looking upward, I saw a magnificent canopy that appeared to arch into the sky. The ceiling was painted to give the illusion of soft, feathery clouds against a background of the bluest sky. The overall effect was breathtaking.

I could not deny that my cousin had built the most awe-inspiring dwelling that my eyes had ever seen. So far, this palace was even more dramatic than any built by our own king. Surely, I thought, Faddel has attained his objective. Paradise could not be more beautiful than this dwelling.

Layla rang a small bell and announced that refreshments would soon be served. She then left us to inform her mistress of our arrival.

I settled on one of the silk divans and patted the spot beside me. 'Come, sit with me in paradise,' I joked.

Maha laughed and sat down.

Amani looked at us sternly as she said, 'Paradise is no joking matter.' She frowned in disapproval as she looked around the extravagant room. 'Anyway, too much sunshine makes a desert.'

I looked around again, with a more critical eye. Amani was right. Faddel's palace was *too* perfect! *Too* beautiful. When the eye sees nothing but perfection, even perfection loses its power to astonish.

Just then four serving girls entered the room. One carried small crystal plates and neatly folded napkins; others held aloft large copper trays heavily laden with food. Delighted, I selected a few sugared almonds, while Maha crowded her plate with tiny sandwiches, delicate cheeses, figs and cherries.

Amani refused every offer of hospitality.

The four servants were all exceptionally pretty and dainty Filipinos. As I stared at those impossibly attractive young women, the idea struck me that Faddel must be truly obsessed with beauty. He seemed determined to surround himself only with beautiful objects, vistas and people. Apparently, he had reached the conclusion that physically unattractive people were not welcome in paradise. I almost laughed aloud when I thought that if a handsome appearance was the criterion for the key to paradise, Faddel was certain to be excluded. God had not blessed Faddel himself with good looks.

Amani startled me when she ran towards the window and squealed, 'Look, there is a family of gazelles grazing on the lawn!'

Indeed, there were four gazelles. Did Faddel have a zoo?

'We'll ask Khalidah to tour the gardens later,' I promised her. 'There might be other animals you can see.'

'I want to see the horses,' Amani said determinedly.

'We shall, daughter.'

I heard a silky rustling sound and looked up to see Khalidah, followed by Layla, entering the room. I had not seen Khalidah for several years, but her beauty had not diminished. In light of Faddel's obvious preoccupation with all things beautiful, I was relieved for her that she was still stunning to look at. Otherwise, she would surely be divorced by her husband.

She was dressed in a gown covered with tiny white pearls, in a shade of green that perfectly set off her chestnut-coloured hair and her amber eyes, which were flecked with gold. Her light-coloured skin was too heavily made up for my liking, but it did nothing to lessen the impact of her lovely features.

I stood and met her embrace.

'Sultana!'

'Khalidah!'

Once our mutual greetings of peace and thanks to Allah for the good fortune of our health were completed, Maha presented Khalidah with our gifts.

Khalidah thanked us profusely and carefully set aside her gifts. She lifted three packages from a gift-laden table, and instructed Layla to deliver them to our driver. We could open our gifts later, after we returned home, she said.

Khalidah apologized that she was alone, explaining that her husband and her six sons were visiting at the palace of a friend, but would soon return. Miraculously, she had given birth only to sons, and for that feat alone she was greatly admired and envied.

Khalidah was anxious to show us her home, and my daughters and I were happy to follow her throughout the vast complex of pavilions. Each pavilion consisted of a small apartment of rooms, each decorated with treasures of unimaginable beauty. My head was soon reeling from the details Khalidah provided us regarding the mosaic floors, wall murals and painted ceilings.

Soon I wanted to escape this profusion of alabaster baths, jewelled vases and silk coverings. I needed air and space, so I suggested that we go outside. 'I have heard much about your beautiful gardens.'

'Yes, of course,' Khalidah agreed amiably. 'Let's sit in the garden.'

Amani reminded me, 'And the stallions, Mother?'

Khalidah reacted strangely to Amani's request. Despite her heavy make-up, her face suddenly turned pale. Her voice trembled, 'Well, that is a domain for men, Amani.'

'I like horses, and I am not a man,' Amani said indignantly.

'Amani!' I warned, as I looked at Khalidah warily. 'We have other places to visit. We will only look at the gardens today.'

I was not that well-acquainted with this cousin, but I knew that few people were accustomed to such an unruly child as Amani.

'Come, let us go to the gardens,' Khalidah said graciously, ignoring my daughter's rude behaviour.

Maha said that she needed to visit the bathroom, and that she would join us later. Layla had returned from her errand, and she led Maha from the room.

I saw that in her anger Amani's lips were now puffed in a most unattractive pout. When she walked beside me, I pinched her arm as a signal that she should hold her temper and her tongue.

Khalidah then led us down a broad pebbled path bordered by a thick hedge. We could see the garden long before we arrived, and as I had expected, it proved to be exquisite. Trees lined the perimeter, and a froth of blooming bushes and flowers grew in every corner. We could smell the strong scent of the flowers' perfume as we strolled through the garden. Terraced flower beds gave way to small ponds filled with exotic fish; a series of carefully constructed brooks bubbled so the soothing sound of running water was all around us. I was truly dazzled.

An artfully designed gazebo caught my eye. 'Can we sit?'

'Certainly, whatever is your pleasure.'

Just as I was about to sit down, Amani gave a small cry. She had noticed cages filled with birds nearby.

I followed her gaze. Small cages, each holding far too many birds, were swinging from the limbs of every tree.

Amani rushed towards the cages.

'You have many birds, Khalidah,' I said uneasily, all the while watching Amani dart frantically from one cage to the next.

Khalidah seemed mesmerized by Amani's small scurrying form. She sounded like one in a trance. 'Yes. Faddel believes that paradise is filled with many songbirds.'

Even at a distance, I could see the fury on Amani's face.

I called out. 'Amani? Amani, please join us, darling.'

With fists clenched in anger, Amani ran towards Khalidah and began shouting, 'Their cages are too small! There's not enough food and water!'

Khalidah appeared momentarily stunned by my daughter's rudeness; words failed her.

'Amani!' I admonished. 'You *must* apologize!'

Tears were streaming down Amani's face. 'Some of the birds are dead!'

I turned to Khalidah and made an attempt to lighten the situation. 'Do not mind Amani. All creatures are a source of endless fascination to my daughter.'

Amani looked at me disdainfully as though I were a traitor. 'The cages are too small! There's not enough food!'

'Amani! I *order* you to apologize. Now!'

In an effort to appease my child, Khalidah stammered, 'But . . . my dear, there are birds in paradise.'

My daughter screamed so loudly that the veins on her neck and forehead were visible under her skin. 'Birds in paradise fly free!'

Khalidah's hands were clutching at her throat.

Amani was becoming hysterical. 'They fly free, I tell you! Birds in paradise fly free! You are cruel to have them so confined!'

'Amani! Enough!' I started towards my daughter, prepared to give her a good shaking. It was time to take her home.

Khalidah kept her hand at her throat and said helplessly, 'But, I tell you, Amani, there *are* birds in paradise. I am sure of it.'

Amani glared at her with hatred. Her voice was filled with contempt. 'You will never find out! Your wicked eyes will never see true paradise!'

Overwhelmed at such unexpected aggression, Khalidah fell over in a faint.

I watched in horror as Amani, seeing her chance, darted from one cage to another. She was removing the cages from the trees!

As I knelt down to try to rouse Khalidah, Maha

came running down the path towards me in a state of agitation. Her voice was loud in indignation. 'Mother, did you know that Cousin Faddel has imprisoned a group of young girls? He has a harem of young women! They are held captive in one of the pavilions!'

Alarmed and shocked, I could only stare at Maha.

It was then that Maha noticed the fallen Khalidah.

'What has happened to Cousin Khalidah?'

I astonished myself with my calm tone. 'Amani insulted her. Khalidah fainted.' I gestured towards the palace. 'Now, go quickly and get some help.'

'But, what about those poor girls?'

'Hush, Maha! We'll deal with that problem later.' I looked down at Khalidah, and was relieved to see that she was still breathing. I ordered Maha, 'Go, get help! Now!'

Maha ran towards the palace, shouting Layla's name.

Amid the turmoil and confusion I saw Amani leave the garden, struggling with an unwieldy load. It took some moments to comprehend that my daughter was in the process of appropriating Faddel's caged birds!

I cried, 'Oh Allah!' I then called out, 'Amani! Amani! Come back!'

Grappling with as many cages as she could possibly carry, Amani disappeared from sight.

Birds of Paradise

I once heard someone say that we do not remember *days* of our lives, but we do remember *moments*. I know it is true, for I have lived such 'peak' moments myself.

Desperation swept through me now, though, as I held Khalidah's head in my lap. I strained to look for Maha, waiting impatiently for her return. Helpless, I could only watch Amani's small body dashing hurriedly back and forth through the garden, on forays collecting birdcages crowded with chirping birds. Such a moment I will never forget!

Maha finally returned to the garden with Layla at her side. Three Egyptian men followed closely behind. I could only assume that these men were servants employed by Faddel.

Layla had already been alerted by Maha of Khalidah's plight, so she quickly rushed to assist me in my so-far-futile efforts to revive her mistress. The three men watched uneasily as they stood silently around the limp figure of Khalidah.

Meanwhile, Amani continued with her urgent task of emptying Faddel's paradise garden of every singing creature. Thankfully, Khalidah's employees were so preoccupied with their mistress's condition that they did not notice the frantic behaviour of my daughter which was taking place behind them.

Khalidah finally opened her eyes and when she saw my face hovering over hers, she groaned and swooned again. After the third time I had roused my cousin only to witness her immediate relapse, I decided that Khalidah should be moved to her bed. I sprang to my feet as I instructed the male servants, 'Quickly, lift your mistress and carry her into the palace.'

All three men exchanged worried glances, and then stepped backward. Their eyes betrayed their thoughts; I saw that they considered me of unsound mind. The smallest of the men finally spoke, 'Madam, it is forbidden.'

Standing there, with the helpless Khalidah at my feet, I realized that these men were repelled by the very thought of touching Khalidah, their mistress, true, but a woman nevertheless.

Many fundamentalist Muslim men believe that all women are impure, and that if they touch even the palm of a woman not legally bound to them, they will suffer red-hot embers applied to their own palms on Judgement Day.

Since it is reported that Prophet Mohammed refused to touch any woman who did not belong to him, there are many *hadiths*, or interpretations, of the Prophet's words and actions on this subject. A popular *hadith* on this very topic is that: 'A praying man may interrupt his prayers if one of three things should pass in front of him: a black dog, a woman or an ass.' On more than one occasion I have even heard my own father say that he would rather be splashed by a pig than to brush against the elbow of a woman that he did not know.

Without thinking, I rushed towards the two men closest to me and simultaneously grabbed both their arms. 'Take your mistress into the palace! Now!'

The two men, with eyes opened wide in alarm, struggled to disengage themselves from my grasp. With a look of genuine shock and repulsion on their faces, both men stooped to the ground and began to rub sand on the skin of their arms where I had touched them.

Their reaction infuriated me. Even though I am aware that the Koran warns that if a man touches a strange woman, and cannot find water to wash, then he should find 'clean' soil and rub away the pollution of that woman, I was still offended.

The quick-thinking Layla intervened. 'Wait,' she said, 'I have an idea.' She rushed back towards the palace.

I turned my attention back to Khalidah. I patted her cheeks and called out her name. She refused to respond to my pleas, but when I turned to address Maha, I saw her peek at me through slightly opened eyelids. Obviously Khalidah was feigning her condition so that she could escape answering Amani's charge of cruelty, and, in the process, gain sympathy.

Layla returned with a blanket which she laid out like a mat next to her mistress. Since these foolish servants still refused to touch her, Layla, Maha and I rolled Khalidah from the grass onto that mat. I then ordered the men to take the corners of the blanket, and still they recoiled. I shrieked that I would have them jailed! Knowing I was of royal blood, each of the men then reluctantly gripped a corner of the blanket. With faces filled with pained endurance, they slowly conveyed the debilitated Khalidah back to the palace.

I ordered Maha to find her sister, who could no longer be seen in the garden, and told her to bring her to me in the palace.

Once Khalidah had revived enough to take tea, I made profuse apologies for the unfortunate incident. My cousin drank her tea in silence, refusing to look at me. But, when I reminded her that many modern children are high-strung and uncontrollable, she gave a slight nod of recognition. I had heard gossip that several of Khalidah's sons were problems and she seemed to have some understanding of having such a defiant child as Amani.

After a sombre farewell, I left the palace without informing Khalidah that Faddel's birds were no longer living in his earthly paradise. My reasoning for this deception was that I had optimistic plans to return these birds before they were missed.

As I walked down the long hallway to the entrance of the palace, Maha rushed towards me. We took each other's hands. Out of breath from her running, she wheezed, 'Amani has disappeared, and so has our driver!'

Taking a deep breath, I almost smiled when I remembered an ancient proverb often repeated to me by my mother. 'Remember, Maha, "no matter how high a bird flies, it is destined to land somewhere". We will find Amani. And, those birds will be with her.'

Questioning Mustafa, the Egyptian doorman, I quickly learned that our own driver had assisted

Amani in gathering Faddel's birds and had then driven my daughter and her illicit cargo away from the palace. Mustafa mentioned that he was surprised that his mistress had given my daughter an Eid gift of so many birds. He whispered behind his hand as if sharing a secret, 'My master and his mistress are very attached to their earthly belongings.'

I looked thoughtfully at this poor man. Clearly, all was not perfect in Faddel's paradise.

In the Islamic religion, there is a great duty for almsgiving, both mandatory and voluntary. For many years, I had heard rumours that Faddel, who was one of the richest Al Sa'uds, always made a great show of paying the obligatory *zakat* (the small percentage of income, like a tithe, required by law of every Muslim) yet refused to contribute a single Saudi riyal voluntarily to charity. In the Arab world, generosity is expected, especially of those who are wealthy, but even poor Arabs are generous to a fault, believing that to receive more than one gives is a great humiliation.

Faddel, however, was evidently a greedy man in satisfying his own desires, while miserly in his dealings with others. Faddel would pay his staff meagre wages, I guessed, and would happily grind the faces of the poor into the desert sand without remorse. Such a man would surely demand the return of the birds that his money had purchased.

As these thoughts raced through my mind, Mustafa arranged for one of Khalidah's drivers to return Maha and me to our own palace. Once we had settled back in the limousine as it moved through the streets of Jeddah, Maha became impatient to bring the subject of the young girls in Faddel's harem to my renewed attention.

Mindful of the driver, I silenced my daughter with a look and a nudge, and whispered, 'Darling, I promise I will hear you out, and we will help those young women, but first, we must return these birds before they are missed.'

The moment my feet touched the driveway in front of our palace, I started calling out for my youngest daughter. 'Amani!'

Three of the Filipino gardeners, Tony, Frank and Jerry looked up from their pruning.

'She went there, ma'am,' Tony said, pointing in the direction of the women's garden.

'We helped her carry many birds, ma'am,' Jerry added.

Good, I thought, I will speak with Amani while the servants are reloading the birdcages.

At that moment, I saw Kareem's automobile slowly wind down our driveway. I steeled myself for what was to come as I watched him emerge from the back seat and walk towards me. He seemed to be in good humour after spending all day with the king and other royal cousins, and smiled cheerfully.

I felt a flicker of sorrow for my husband, knowing that his good temperament would soon dissipate. I raised my eyebrows in greeting, but did not smile or speak when he squeezed my hand.

Kareem knows me well. 'What is the problem, Sultana?'

'You will never believe what I have to tell you,' I said, wearily.

As I confided the afternoon's troubles at the

palace of Faddel, Kareem's face turned several shades of red as his anger grew.

'And, now, Amani is in the garden with the birds,' I concluded.

Kareem stood speechless as he tried to grasp the consequences of his daughter stealing a large number of birds from a royal cousin.

The persistent ringing of Kareem's cellular telephone interrupted our fretful thoughts, and to my irritation, Kareem answered the phone. The conversation was not to his liking, for his face turned even redder.

'Yes,' he said in a calm voice. 'What you have heard is correct. Yes. I will attend to the matter now.' Kareem gave me a pointed look.

'Who was that?'

'Faddel wants those damn birds returned. Immediately.'

I groaned. No more than an hour had passed, and Faddel already knew about Amani's mischief! My plan to return the birds quietly was no longer possible.

Just then Maha came running from the women's garden. 'Mother, Amani she says she'll kill herself before she lets you take away the birds!'

I slapped my hands together.

'I think she means it, too,' Maha added melodramatically. 'She claims she will garrotte herself with her red leather belt!'

I screamed.

With a worried look, Kareem headed for the women's garden. Maha and I followed him without a word. So did Tony, Frank and Jerry, at a discreet distance.

Amani was standing guard in front of the lines

of birdcages. A determined look was etched on her face, and her eyes glowered.

Kareem was furious but he spoke cautiously. 'Amani, I have just received a disturbing telephone call from Cousin Faddel. He told me an unbelievable story. He says that you, Amani, stole his birds. Is this true, daughter?'

Amani moved her lips into a smile, but the look in her eyes negated it. 'I did save some birds from a terrible death, Father.'

Kareem said calmly, 'You know you must return those birds, daughter. They do not belong to you.'

My eyes were fixed pleadingly on Amani, hoping she would consent.

Amani's phoney smile disappeared. She thought for a moment before tilting her head in defiance. In a clear and sure voice, she quoted a verse of the Koran, 'And they feed, for the love of God, the indigent, the orphan and the captive.' And added, in her own words, 'The righteous Muslim will not starve any animal.'

Every Muslim knows that Islamic authorities agree that the word 'captive' includes animals who are under subjection to man, and that such creatures must be properly fed, housed and looked after by faithful Muslims.

'You will have to return the birds, Amani,' Kareem repeated sternly.

A strangled scream burst out of Amani. 'There was no food or water in many of the cages!' Her hoarse voice lowered as she turned to stare into one of the cages nearest her. 'When I looked into their sweet little faces, I knew that I must save them!' She gestured towards a bench behind her. 'I was too late to save them all,' she said, her voice quivering. 'I found more than two dozen dead birds.'

I looked at the bench and was startled to see a large number of dead birds lying in a perfect row. Amani had placed a wreath of freshly picked flowers around the tiny bodies.

Tears began to form in her eyes. 'I will give them a funeral later,' Amani promised.

The insensitive Maha laughed loudly, echoed by the three Filipino gardeners.

'Shut up and leave this place,' Kareem commanded angrily.

Maha shrugged, and then turned away, but the sound of her amused laughter followed her as she walked down the garden path.

The three Filipinos took cover behind some bushes. I did not point out their presence to Kareem because they were three of my favourite servants, and I did not want to risk deflecting Kareem's great anger towards Amani onto them. The lives of our unmarried servants are so empty of family life that they tend to take great interest in our household dramas.

Amani was weeping in earnest now. 'I will not return these birds!' she pledged. 'If you force me to do so, I will throw myself into the Red Sea!'

I gasped, first the garrotte and now the sea! How would I ever protect my child from the force of her own emotions?

Kareem's voice sounded drained and tired. 'Amani, sweetheart, I will buy you a thousand other birds.'

'No! No! I will not return these birds!' Amani flung her small body over one of the birdcages and began to screech.

Distraught, Kareem and I both ran to her side.

'Darling,' I cried, 'you are going to make yourself sick. Hush, little one.' Amani's sobs were coming from deep inside her body. I had heard of a female cousin who had cried so hysterically at the sight of her deceased mother that she had broken a blood vessel in her throat and had nearly joined her mother in the grave! I now had horrific visions of such a thing happening to my own daughter. Never had I seen Amani so tormented.

Kareem lovingly held the child in his arms. 'All right, Amani. You can keep these birds. I will buy Faddel some more.'

This idea did not meet with Amani's approval either. She screamed, 'No! Would you provide the murderer with new victims?'

Kareem held tight to his child. He and I exchanged a look of despair. He took her small face in his large hands as he pleaded, 'Amani, if you will only stop crying, I promise you, I will think of something we can do.'

Amani's wild cries slowly turned into pitiful whimpers. Kareem gathered his child in his arms and carried her into the palace and to her room. While Kareem comforted Amani, I searched her room and removed every item that could possibly be used to inflict self-injury. I also removed every sharp or pointed object from her bathroom. Amani did not seem to notice.

On the way back to Amani's room, I ordered Maha to assist our female servants in making a sweep of our palace. Until this crisis passed, I wanted anything that could be used as a harmful weapon to be locked away.

Maha began to grumble that we were willing to

save Faddel's stupid birds but did not care that young girls were being held there against their will. It was true that I had forgotten all about Maha's claim to have discovered a harem of distressed girls. I now assured my daughter, 'Maha, give your father and me time to calm this situation. After that, I promise, I will check to see what is happening with those young women.'

When Maha made an ugly face and began to make fun of her sister, my patience snapped. 'Hush, now! You know how Amani feels when it comes to animals. How would you feel if your sister slashed her throat or hanged herself?'

'I would prepare a feast and hold a great party,' Maha snarled.

I slapped her twice and she became contrite and hurried to do my bidding.

When I returned to Amani's room, my wonderful husband was patiently making a list of Amani's immediate demands for the care of the rescued birds. He obviously sensed, as did I, that Amani was dangerously close to a nervous collapse.

Kareem turned to me and held out the list. 'Sultana, send one of the drivers to purchase twenty large birdcages, a variety of bird seed and any bird treats and toys that the store might stock.'

'Yes, of course,' I murmured. As my eyes scanned the list, I did Kareem's bidding. Within the hour, two of our drivers had returned from pet shops in the city; both had cleaned out the stock in those stores of everything intended for the care of birds.

Kareem instructed all six of our gardeners to lay aside their normal tasks and help move the birds from their small cages into the new, larger ones. Only after Amani inspected the birds and saw for herself that these creatures were properly fed, watered and housed in large cages, did she agree to sleep.

I was still apprehensive, so I arranged for six servants to take turns watching over my child while she slept.

Maha, still angry over the events of the day, refused to join us for the evening meal. Kareem and I were too emotionally exhausted to care, and we sat in silence as we ate our light meal of chicken kebabs over rice.

Faddel called Kareem on the telephone three times while we were eating, but Kareem refused to take his calls. Only after our meal did he telephone him back to assure him that he would visit Faddel the following day.

Kareem then informed the cook that we would take our coffee in the women's gardens, where we sat at a table under one of the trees. Although it was nearly dark, the lively sounds of fluttering birds chirping and splashing in bird baths created a noisy commotion that was difficult to ignore. But I listened with pleasure to the birds enjoying their new lives.

A look from Kareem led to my moving from my chair into his lap. I knew that Kareem's thoughts were as mine: if we returned those birds, Amani was fully capable of doing harm to herself. Yet, if we purchased new birds to replace the ones she had stolen, Amani would certainly discover our deception. On the other hand, Faddel was not the type to yield. What on earth were we going to do?

I whispered, 'Do you have a plan, Kareem?'

Kareem sighed, but did not speak for a long moment. Finally, he said, 'That Faddel is a greedy bastard. I have decided to deed him a piece of my prime property in Riyadh, *if* he will agree to forgo having birds of any kind in his ridiculous paradise. *That* should make Amani happy.'

'Prime real estate for a bunch of bedraggled songbirds! Oh, Allah. We will become a big joke!'

'No. Faddel will not speak of this. Not only is he greedy, he is a coward. I will make it clear that it would not be in his best interest to spread news of our private business.'

'He is an evil man,' I agreed, suddenly remembering what Maha had claimed to have found out. I was tempted to ask Kareem if he knew anything about Faddel's private harem, but I quickly decided that my poor husband had already heard enough problems for one day.

As we sat under the trees, suddenly, at the same moment, every bird in the garden began to sing. Kareem and I sat quietly listening, overcome by the beauty of the sound.

Later, after enjoying our coffee, we retired to our quarters. The long day had finally come to an end, and for that I was most grateful. When I remembered my promise to Maha, however, I had difficulty getting to sleep. Today's events had drained me of all energy. What would a new morning bring?

Heavenly Harem

When I opened my eyes the following morning, I found myself alone in bed. I called out Kareem's name, but there was no response. My mind was so disordered that it took some minutes for the events of the previous day to come flooding back. Amani – and her birds! This was why Kareem had awakened so early; the bird business with Faddel would certainly be his first priority today.

I slipped on a simple cotton dress before leaving my suite. First, I paused at Maha's door and listened. There was no sound, which was a good sign. If Maha were awake, ear-splitting music would reverberate through the door. It was my wish that Maha sleep through the noon hour. I needed time alone to work out an appropriate response to the allegedly captive girls' plight, and to prevent our household from plunging into yet another crisis that involved Faddel.

With a sigh, I pushed that unpleasant thought out of my mind as I walked towards Amani's room. My youngest daughter was still sleeping. One of the six Filipino housemaids that I had assigned to watch over her was sitting by her bedside, and she reassured me, 'Ma'am, your daughter slept peacefully throughout the night.'

I retraced my steps back to my own quarters before ordering coffee and a light breakfast of yogurt, cheese and flat bread from the kitchen. In contrast to yesterday's dreadful upheavals, there was time for delicious idleness. I lazily stirred my coffee while sitting on our private terrace and enjoyed the spectacular view over the Red Sea which our Jeddah palace offered. It was a day fit for a god. The sky was cloudless and blue, and rays of the sun were warm, not hot, at this hour. Bands of sunlight penetrated deeply into the crystalline waters of the Red Sea. Watching the slow-moving waves lap softly against the shoreline, my body soon fell in rhythm with the sea. If only all days could be as peaceful as this.

Before I had finished my breakfast, Kareem returned. He settled down in the chair beside me and began to pick at my food with his fingers.

In silence, I examined Kareem's handsome face, stretching out the minutes of tranquillity as long as possible.

'Tell me,' I finally said.

Kareem brought his eyebrows together and then wearily shook his head. 'That bastard, Faddel, claimed to have developed a special affection for those damn birds.'

'He would not trade the birds for land?' I asked in disbelief.

Kareem's eyebrows lifted. 'Of course he would, Sultana. But, he was deliberately difficult.'

'Tell me everything.'

'I do not wish to relive every detail, Sultana,' he said impatiently. 'All you need to know is we now own cousin Faddel's birds, or rather, Amani does.

And I have Faddel's assurances that songbirds will no longer be brought into his earthly paradise.' Kareem lowered his voice slightly. 'I'm convinced the man is a lunatic. Can Faddel truly believe that he can outwit God by experiencing paradise without death?' Kareem shook his head back and forth in wonder. 'A lunatic.'

I smiled gratefully at my husband. 'At least Amani will be consoled. Not many fathers would go to such extremes for the happiness of their children.' I leaned towards my husband and playfully kissed his lips.

But Kareem's expression hardened. 'Sultana, those cousins have never been our friends, so I do not understand why you chose to visit them in the first place. Please, for the benefit of all, from now on stay away from that family.'

I tried to keep my emotions from showing in my face. I desperately wanted to tell Kareem about Maha's shocking claim about a harem with girls kept against their will, and if it were true, my urgent need to help them. But, I could not speak, for this was not the time. I knew that my husband would consider the fate of the captive women outside the realm of our influence. He was certain to forbid my interference.

So when Kareem took my arm, looked deeply in my eyes, and said, 'Stay away from Faddel and Khalidah. Do you understand, Sultana?' I just nodded and muttered, '*Wala yoldaghul moumenu min juhren marratayn*,' which means: 'The believer never gets a second snake bite from the same snake hole.'

Satisfied that he had made his point, Kareem stood up and put on his most serious face. 'We must be wise when choosing our acquaintances, Sultana. Any association with such people as Faddel can only lead to unpleasant consequences.'

He paused, then said, 'I am thinking of visiting Hanan and Mohammed. Would you like to come?'

'Thank you, but no. It's best that I remain with our daughters this day. But, please, darling, will you take along the Eid gifts that I purchased for them?'

I cared deeply for Hanan, who was Kareem's youngest sister, and her husband Mohammed. Actually, apart from Kareem's mother, Noorah, I liked every member of my husband's family, and I looked forward to our visits together with delight. As the years passed, I came to realize that I was fortunate indeed to be married into a family like Kareem's.

Kareem left our palace, and, after a bath, I went to inform Amani of her father's good news. The poor girl was still in bed and in a deep sleep. The previous day had been so trying for her! Looking at Amani's sleeping form, I was overcome with love for her, despite her sharp tongue. I kissed her lightly on the cheek before I left to find Maha.

With Amani's crisis behind me, I now knew that I must pay attention to Maha's story to maintain my daughter's respect, and my own self-respect as a champion of women's rights.

Maha was up and getting dressed. To my surprise, she was not listening to music. Her eyes met mine in the reflection of her vanity mirror. I could see that she was still angry about the previous day's incident.

'What happened to those birds?' she asked in a surly tone.

Cautiously, I said, 'Your father handled the problem. The birds now belong to Amani.'

Maha made an exasperated face. 'How did Father manage *that*?'

'Your father made Faddel a rather generous offer,' I admitted.

Maha's lip curled. 'Well, I refuse to attend a bird funeral! I mean it, Mother!'

I gently placed my hand on Maha's shoulder and spoke to her image in the mirror. 'If that is your wish, Maha.'

She jerked her shoulder away from my touch.

I knew that an apology was in order. I sighed as I said, 'Darling, I am sorry about yesterday. Truly, I am, but to hear you say such cruel and unfeeling things about your sister drove me mad. Believe me, should real harm come to Amani, the last thing you would do is to feast and dance.' I paused for a moment before adding, 'If a tragedy should really strike Amani, your heart would be for ever burdened by your thoughtless words.'

After considering my words, Maha's fury seemed to vanish. She smiled. 'You are right, Mother.' She swivelled around on her vanity stool, and stared intently into my face. 'Now, can we go and save those young women at Cousin Faddel's palace?'

I sighed deeply. I, too, had once been aflame with the overwhelming desire to help every woman in need. I patted Maha's cheek lovingly before sitting down on her bed.

'Darling, tell me about the young women. How did you learn about them?'

Maha laid aside her powder brush and turned to look at me. Her voice started to race and she stumbled over her words. 'All right, Mother, I will tell you. Yesterday, after I came out of the bathroom at that evil palace, Layla was nowhere to be found. Since I did not know where the garden was located, I began to walk around the grounds, looking for you. I searched everywhere, and soon became lost in that maze of pavilions! I found myself on the path leading to the horses, and thought that the gardens might be in that area.'

Maha scooted her vanity stool along the floor towards me. She took my hands and squeezed them between her own. 'Mother, Cousin Faddel does not own any horses! That sign led to a pavilion filled with beautiful young women!'

I had to think for a minute before it struck me. Stallions! I understood that the sign was Faddel's idea of a joke – a joke at the expense of innocent young women, no doubt.

'Perhaps these women chose what they are doing?' I suggested tentatively. I know that the poverty in other countries often drives young girls, or their families, to agree to sell their bodies.

'No! No!' Maha vigorously shook her head back and forth. 'Several of these young women threw themselves at my feet and pleaded with me to save them!' Maha's eyes began to fill with tears. 'Some of them can be no more than twelve or thirteen years old!'

I cried out in anguish. These girls were younger even than Amani.

'What did you tell them?'

'I promised them that I would come back, and soon! That I would bring my mother to them, and that she would know what to do.'

'Oh, Maha.' I closed my eyes and let my chin

fall onto my chest. 'If only life were so simple.'

With a sinking feeling, I began to recall the number of times that I, too, had been as idealistic and optimistic as my daughter. Now, as a woman of forty, I knew that it was not a simple matter to come between men and their sexual desires. It is the natural inclination of many men, and not only in the Middle East, to seek out young girls or young women as sexual conquests. And too often it seems to be of no concern to them that their pleasure is taken from one who is too young, or who is forced against her will.

'What a cruel and evil world we live in,' I said dejectedly, as tears filled my eyes.

Maha looked at me trustingly. 'What are you going to do, Mother? I promised them!'

I made a painful admission. 'I do not know, Maha. I do not know.'

'Perhaps Father can help,' Maha said, with hope reflected in her innocent face. 'Just as he saved Amani's birds!'

I sat silently, fighting the irresistible force of our reality. I recalled clearly a time in the late 1980s when Cory Aquino, then President of the Philippines, had made a diplomatic issue out of young Filipino girls being hired to come as housemaids to Saudi Arabia but when they arrived being forced to serve as sex slaves. Aquino had banned single Filipino women from travelling to Saudi Arabia.

Our own King Fahd had become furious at this insulting restriction and reacted with a ban of his own, saying that all Filipinos, both male and female, would be forbidden from working in Saudi Arabia if President Aquino's ban was enforced. Aquino's brave attempt to protect her countrywomen was a failure, for the economy of her country greatly depended upon Filipino people working in the oil-rich lands of the Middle East and sending their money back to support their families. And so young Filipino women hired as housemaids still serve our men as sex slaves, in addition to their household duties.

'Mother?'

I searched my mind for a solution, but, once more, I had to admit, 'I do not know what to do.'

'If Father can free a bunch of birds, why can't he do the same for human beings?'

'Your father has gone for the day.'

'Then, Mother, we shall go there. We will bring those girls back here, and we will hire them to work as our maids!' she said passionately.

'Maha, it is more complicated than that.'

Maha jumped to her feet with pain and fury on her face. 'I will go alone, then! Like Amani, I will free these girls by myself!'

Knowing that my daughter had made up her mind, I realized I had no choice.

'All right, Maha. We will go together.'

I informed my Filipino maid, Letha, that we were leaving, instructing her that the moment Amani awakened, she should tell her that the birds now belonged to her. Then I accompanied Maha back to 'Paradise Palace', not knowing what to expect.

Once we had arrived on Faddel's palace grounds, I told our driver, 'We are meeting Khalidah outside the palace.' I pointed to the 'Stallions' sign. 'Please drop us off here, return to the gate and await our summons.' Both the driver and I carried cellular telephones.

A sceptical look passed across the driver's face, but he did as he was instructed.

Maha and I both fell silent as we walked down that long pathway. We were both aware that we were involving ourselves in a very serious matter. And all without Kareem's knowledge.

Soon I saw the infamous pavilion, standing alone, just as Maha had described it. To me, this building seemed identical to the other pavilions except that, upon closer inspection, I saw that the windows were barred.

'How can we get inside?' I whispered, certain that this building was securely locked.

'The door is unlocked,' Maha told me, to my disbelief. 'I asked the girls why they did not run away. I was told that several girls had done so, but without their passports and the appropriate travel papers signed by a Saudi man, they were always brought back to certain punishment and even worse treatment.'

'Hmmm.' I could understand this. Unfortunately, most people in Saudi Arabia, expatriates and native citizens alike, would be too fearful of retaliation to offer help to any woman claiming she was being held in sexual bondage. Few people will risk imprisonment for the sake of a stranger, and the men of my family often take revenge upon people who expose the dark side of life in Saudi Arabia.

As we neared the pavilion, a very old and bizarre-looking little man stepped out of the bushes and in front of our path. We were both so shocked at his appearance that we screamed.

Gasping for breath, I stood without speaking as I took in this most unusual creature. He was short and skinny and ebony black. He appeared shorter than he was by an unfortunate forward curvature of the spine. His withered face showed his extreme age. His skin hung in loose folds around his jowls. Yes, I decided, this was indeed the most ancient person I had ever seen.

Despite his age, though, he was dressed in a bright yellow blouse and a sequined red vest. A silk turban, turquoise in colour, was wound around his head. His full-cut trousers, fashioned out of a rich brocade run through with golden threads, suggested the costume of another age.

'May I help you, madam?' The man's voice was abnormally high-pitched. And, kindly!

I looked more closely into his face and saw brown eyes that were sparkling with curiosity.

'Madam?' He waved one small black hand before my eyes.

I noted that he wore a ring on every finger.

'Who are you?' I managed to sputter.

'I am Omar,' he said, with great pride. 'Omar, of the Sudan.'

For the first time I noticed that the old man's face was as hairless as my own. Suddenly I was struck with a thought. Was I looking at a eunuch? I wondered. Surely, there were no longer eunuchs in Saudi Arabia!

In the not so distant past, there were many eunuchs in Arabia. Although the Islamic faith forbids Muslims to castrate young boys themselves, Muslims were not forbidden from owning eunuchs as slaves. In fact, my forebears considered eunuchs as prized possessions, and paid huge sums for them. Once, eunuchs guarded the harems of wealthy Arabs. And they were also a common sight in the mosques of Makkah and Medina, where they were assigned to separate the women from the men when they entered the mosques.

Here I was actually looking at one of these eunuchs, now pitifully aged. I was certain of it.

Acid words came to my tongue, for I was immediately convinced of the role of this little man here at Faddel's pavilion. 'And, I suppose you guard Faddel's harem?'

Omar chuckled lightly. 'No, Madam, I do not.' He pinched the loose flesh hanging from his arm. 'I could only guard prisoners who are volunteers, nothing more.'

As I looked down at his small shrunken figure I saw his point.

He explained. 'Faddel's father was once my master; his son allows me to continue to live here.'

Maha had soon overcome her fear of the little man. She now impatiently tugged on my arm. 'Mother! Please hurry!'

Omar's appearance had taken me back to another time, and I was curious to ask this eunuch many questions, but the compelling reason for my visit here took precedence. I must find the imprisoned women before I was discovered by Faddel. My only hope was that the eunuch would not alert Faddel and Khalidah of our unauthorized entry into the grounds.

'We are here only to speak to the young women living there,' I pointed at the pavilion. 'We will not be long. You have my word.'

Omar swept his head to the ground in a graceful bow. 'You are most welcome.'

Enchanted at his display of gracious manners, I smiled as Maha and I brushed past him.

The moment we stepped into the interior of the pavilion, we were surrounded by a large number of excited young women. Most looked Asian. Maha was greeted with many hugs and kisses. Happy voices rang out in the room. 'You kept your word! We will be freed!'

I cautioned them. 'Quiet! You will wake those already in the grave!'

The loud laughing voices became low, joyful voices.

I took a moment to survey Faddel's harem while the anxious young women swirled around Maha with many questions. Surprisingly, considering Faddel's preoccupation with all things beautiful, the room where we stood appeared rather shabby. Although the furniture was expensive and the walls were covered in gold silk, the ornate decorations appeared garish and grubby. Stacks of videotapes and ashtrays piled high with cigarette butts and ash cluttered the room.

I looked closely at the young girls. Each one was beautiful, but their tawdry attire drew the eye to more than their beauty. Some were dressed in Western-style halter-tops and jeans; others wore sheer nighties. There was nothing glamorous about their harem apparel. Sadly, all of them were unbearably young.

While most of the girls were Asian, I saw one who appeared to be Arab. Several were smoking cigarettes and sipping cold drinks. I had never imagined that a harem and its occupants could appear so conspicuously vulgar. However, I imagined that to Faddel's eyes, these young women were like the seductive virgins called 'houris' that are described in the Koran. I suspected that I was looking at a stage intended to provide untold delights for Faddel. Yet this must be the scene of unspeakable hell for these women held against their will.

'Everyone, quickly, sit down,' I ordered, as I retrieved a pen and pad from within my large handbag. 'We do not have much time,' I said, as I looked towards the door at the entrance of the pavilion. I gasped when I saw that Omar had followed Maha and me, and was now sitting comfortably on the carpeted floor. He smiled broadly. However, some inner sense told me that I had no reason to fear the little man.

'Now, I am going to pass this notebook around the room. Everyone, please write down your name, and an address where I can reach your relatives.'

A low moan of disappointment and frustration swept through the room. One of the older girls, whom I judged to be about twenty years old, asked me in her soft voice, 'Then, we are not going with you *today*, ma'am?'

Sadly, with my hand I made a sweeping motion around the room. 'I cannot. Look at you, you are too many. I have no way of obtaining passports. You would be returned before nightfall.' I paused as I quickly counted. There were twenty-five young girls in that room. I then tried to speak above the din of their voices.

'Your families must protest to their embassies. That is your best chance for release.'

Sobbing voices began to clamour in objection.

One of the younger girls, who disclosed that she was from Thailand, wailed, 'But, ma'am, my own parents sold me to this man.' Her sobbing voice drifted off. 'They will not help me . . .'

'That is my story too,' said another girl, shivering in her skimpy outfit. 'I was taken from my small village in the north to Bangkok. My brother collected many American dollars for me.'

Another frightened girl said, 'I believed that I had been hired to work as a maid! But, it was all a lie!'

'And, I? I was employed as a seamstress in a factory. My days were spent sewing; my nights were spent serving many men. I was sold to three different men before being purchased by Master Faddel.'

Trying to collect my bewildered thoughts, I exchanged a glance with Maha. If the families of these young girls had actually sold them into slavery, how could I possibly help them?

'Let me think,' I said nervously. 'I need to think.'

A delicate young beauty, her eyes tear-filled, lightly touched my arm. 'You *must* take us with you! If you only knew my story, you would not leave me here, not for another moment!'

Looking into the sad eyes of that young woman, my heart broke. Although I was fearful of wasting time, I listened quietly.

Encouraged by my silence, the young woman said, 'I am from a large family in Laos. My family was starving, so when two men from Bangkok offered money to take me with them, my parents had no choice. I was chained together with three other girls from my village, and then we were taken to Bangkok. We were unloaded at a large warehouse. Then we were forced to stand naked on a platform before a room filled with men. We were sold at auction. The other two girls were purchased by a brothel owner, but I was bought by a man representing Arabs. And, that is how I came to be here, ma'am.' Her voice grew low in a pitiful plea. 'Please do not leave me here.'

This story stunned me into silence. Women were being sold at *auctions*, to the *highest bidders*?

Omar interrupted, 'Why not take these girls with you today, mistress? Leave them at their embassies. They can take shelter there, I believe.'

What Omar said was true. I recalled a London television news report of maltreated Filipino maids in neighbouring Kuwait who had taken refuge in just such a manner. Although the Kuwaiti government had denied their stories of mistreatment, and forced these young women to live in limbo for many months, eventually they had been given their freedom to return to their home countries.

I smiled once again at Omar. I had hoped he would not be a foe, but I had never dreamed that he would be such an ally.

Soft voices mingled together in a demand for freedom. 'Yes! Yes! Take us today!'

A small, pretty girl with Arabic features inched closer to me. 'Please, help us, ma'am. Our master is a cruel man. He and four of his six sons come to us every day. Oftentimes, he brings many other bad men with him.'

'Our life here is too horrible,' another girl said as she looked beseechingly into my face. 'You cannot imagine what we endure, ma'am.'

I took a deep breath. Should I try to save these girls, no matter the consequences? One look at Maha's face answered my question. Yes, I should!

But, first, I must form a plan. I looked at the girls around me. Many were scantily dressed. I could not take them on the streets of conservative Saudi Arabia in such attire. Angry, rock-throwing crowds would gather, which would ensure failure. 'Do you have cloaks to cover your bodies?'

Several of the girls exchanged looks. One said, 'There are none here that we know of.'

'Use the sheets from the beds,' Omar suggested, giving me a sly, knowing look. 'There are ample beds to provide many covers.'

I glanced at opened doors surrounding the harem. Most led into small cubicles that held beds.

While the girls ran from room to room collecting sheets and bed covers, some of the smallest girls gathered around me. I was astonished to see that two of these girls were mere children! One was no more than eight or nine years old!

I held these children tightly, fighting back rage and tears. How could any mother sell her own daughter? It was utterly unthinkable.

My head was spinning. I knew that I could not transport all twenty-five girls in one automobile. Despite the risk to this secret mission, I must call home and arrange for several other drivers to meet me at Faddel's palace.

I motioned to my daughter. 'Maha, take these children and find covers for them.' When Maha took the children from my arms, I retrieved my cellular phone from my bag, but my chance to make that call never came.

The room erupted in chaos when Faddel, Khalidah and three large men walked into the room. I felt a deadly chill in my veins as I looked into Faddel's cold eyes.

'When we heard the uproar, we had no idea that we had such a distinguished guest,' Faddel said with a smirk as he pulled the telephone from my frozen fingers. 'Sultana, you are not welcome here. Leave this place, at once.'

I looked past Faddel to Khalidah. The last time I had seen Khalidah she had fainted. She looked completely calm now.

'Surely, Khalidah, you do not approve of this.'

Khalidah looked at me with contempt. 'It is not for you, Sultana, to say what goes on in another man's home.'

When the young women realized what was happening, a chorus of screams rang throughout the room. Faddel made a quick motion with his hand. The three burly men accompanying him began to push the young women into rooms and lock them away.

'Maha!' I shouted as I looked around wildly. 'Come here, now!' The idea that my daughter might be locked in with these poor women brought me to the verge of hysterics.

I grabbed Maha's hands as soon as I found her. Once she was safely by my side, I began to plead with Khalidah, hoping she would support the cause of women, her sisters.

'Khalidah, you must know that these young girls are being raped repeatedly – by your husband, sons and other men!' I paused. 'And surely, as a wife and mother, this cannot be to your liking?'

On the surface, Khalidah was stunningly beautiful, but her words today proved to me that she was ugly inside. Worse, she was emotionally and spiritually dead.

She appeared to be unmoved by my words. 'Sultana, this business concerns men only.'

'If you truly believe that, Khalidah, then you are nothing more than a reed in the wind, with no mind of your own.'

Khalidah's face reddened, but she did not respond to my challenge.

I had heard the rumour some years before that Khalidah's attraction to Faddel's enormous wealth was the cause for her blind obedience and loyalty. I longed to shout at Khalidah, to remind her of the wise proverb, 'She who marries a gorilla for money, when the money goes, the gorilla remains a gorilla.' Life is indeed strange, and the day might come when Khalidah found herself with a destitute Faddel whose wickedness would prove more permanent than his wealth.

But I said nothing, aware that such words would not further the cause of freedom for these young women.

Faddel had the effrontery to try to justify his evil deeds. 'Although it is no business of yours, Sultana, every woman here was sold by her parents. They received what they were after, as did I. These transactions were legitimate. I have done nothing wrong.'

'Legally perhaps not, Faddel. Morally, most certainly.'

Faddel shrugged.

Stung by the knowledge I was not going to succeed in freeing these young women, I intentionally insulted my cousin. 'Faddel, is it so terribly difficult for you to find sexual companions who don't have to be chained first?'

Maha turned to him in scorn. 'You are a wicked beast! You are!'

Faddel chuckled when he retorted, 'Sultana, I believe that you and your daughters are conspiring to blacken my reputation.'

Maha grabbed me by the waist. 'Mother! Surely we cannot leave them here?'

My heart sank as I looked into Maha's face. 'Yes, daughter, we must. There is nothing more that we can do here.' I pulled her along. 'Come.'

Khalidah turned her back and left the room.

Faddel's deceptively soft voice spoke menacing words as he guided Maha and me out of that place. 'You know, Sultana, if you were anyone else, I would have you killed.'

Walking beside that depraved man, I felt greater hatred than I had ever felt for any person, even my brother Ali. How I longed to threaten Faddel with a million curses. But I knew that the law of Saudi Arabia had no provisions to help those girls. There was nothing that I could do. Most hurtful of all, Faddel knew it, too.

As we walked away, I heard the heartbroken cries of the young girls, calling out from behind locked doors. It was more than I could bear! I could not imagine how this was affecting Maha.

Dismal thoughts flooded my thinking. Oh, Allah! What a land! What a people! We are so wealthy that we give no thought to exchanging expensive real estate for a nest of motley birds that will satisfy the crazy whims of our children. Yet, we are so morally corrupt that young women are routinely held captive as sex slaves, and incredibly, there are no legal means available for decent people to free these women. I felt hot with shame for my country and my countrymen.

Faddel summoned our driver. He was careful to wait by our side until he saw us off. When our car appeared, Faddel opened the door, returned my cellular telephone, and bade us an ironic farewell. 'You must come again, Sultana.' He chuckled, 'But, please, come to the main house instead.'

Sometimes the defeats in life seem beyond human endurance. I could not speak, and I could not think until I was free of Faddel's loathsome presence.

Maha began to weep. I was too heartsick to offer comforting words, and just gently stroked her shoulder.

As we reached the first turn in the driveway, the eunuch Omar stepped in front of our automobile. Our driver slammed on the brakes. Flashing his toothless smile, Omar tapped on the window.

'Open the window!' I ordered.

'Mistress, might I come with you?' Omar asked in his high feminine voice.

'With me? I thought you were a part of Faddel's family.'

'I said I was *allowed* to live here, madam; I did not say I was *welcomed*.' He added, 'I have not been truly welcome since Faddel's father died, over fifteen years ago.'

'Well . . .' I glanced in the front mirror and saw that the driver was looking at me in alarm. I turned back to Omar. 'Were you bought as a slave by Faddel's family?'

'Slaves were freed many years ago.'

That was true. In 1962 the American President, John F. Kennedy personally appealed to Faisal, who was then Prime Minister, to abolish slavery in Saudi Arabia. Our government honoured President Kennedy's request and purchased freedom for every slave in the country for a price of nearly 5,000 Saudi riyals ($1,500) per head. Many of these freed slaves had remained in their ex-owners' households. Even though Omar had chosen to remain with the family who once owned him, he was his own master.

'Please, mistress.'

I quickly considered this unusual request. Perhaps Faddel would punish Omar for failing to report my arrival at his harem. I now knew him to be perfectly capable of any heinous act.

Reluctantly, I said, 'Well, get in. Come with us.'

Once the little man was settled, I asked, 'What makes you want to live with my family?'

Omar studied me carefully for a moment before answering. 'Well,' he finally said, 'I have lived for many years in this land. When I was eight years old, I was stolen from my family in Sudan and sold to a wealthy Turk. That same year, my owner travelled to Makkah for the haj.' Omar chuckled. 'He was a fat fool who ate too much grease and sugar, and he dropped dead while circling that black rock at the big mosque. I was taken away by the authorities before being presented as a gift to Faddel's grandfather, who was owed some favour or another by the authorities.

'I am now eighty-eight years old. So, for eighty years, I have lived among you people.' He sat silent for a long moment before saying, 'It used to be that Arabs from this country had a little humanity in their hearts. But I have not personally witnessed a single act of kindness in more years than I can remember.' He took a deep breath. 'I promised myself some years ago that the next kind person I met, I would serve.' Omar looked at me and smiled gaily.

The reality of what I had done then came to me. My husband was an indulgent man, but what he was going to say when he saw this fantastically dressed eunuch was something I could not imagine.

When we arrived at our palace, Maha ran weeping to her room.

I told Omar to wait for me in the main living room. He happily complied.

I searched for Amani, and, as I knew I would, I found her in the garden with her birds. I stood and watched my daughter as she indulged her birds with special seeds and treats. Well, at least these particular birds would suffer no more. The garden was filled with their joyous singing.

I drew a sharp breath as I considered my victories and my defeats. The songbirds were free, while the young girls were still captive!

When Kareem arrived home and found me sitting in the living room chatting with the tiny black eunuch, he stared and threw me a look of total incredulity. Poor man! He had no idea of what had transpired that day during his absence. Nor did he know that he now had a eunuch as a part of his household.

The Story of a Eunuch

Many times I have heard Kareem declare that God moves in mysterious ways. Now seeing him reel towards me in a shocked stupor, I hoped to soften what I knew would be my husband's incensed reaction by reminding him of his past assertion. 'Kareem, I now know the true meaning of your wise words. God *does* move in mysterious ways.' I turned from him and smiled at the eunuch. 'God, Himself, has brought Omar of Sudan to live in our home.'

Kareem's automatic Arab hospitality momentarily restrained the anger directed towards me. He looked at the strange little man sitting at my side and greeted him courteously. 'You are most welcome in our home, Omar.'

I tried to bewitch Kareem with my enthusiasm. 'Darling! Omar's story is a legend from our past!'

Kareem showed his scepticism as he inspected Omar's colourful ensemble. 'Oh?'

I did not want Kareem to judge Omar harshly, for I understood that this small man had not chosen the role in life he had been forced to play.

'Yes! Omar's lifelong mission has been that of a protector. A protector of women!'

Just then Amani walked into the palace with a row of her new pet birds balanced on her arm. Miraculously, our daughter had already trained some of the birds she had saved from Faddel's garden paradise.

With a broad smile on his face, Omar jumped to his feet. 'Young mistress, I watched from the bushes as you carried these poor birds from Master Faddel's palace to freedom. For sure, you will be favoured by Allah for your goodness!'

Amani had never been praised for protecting animals before. Disarmed, she smiled warmly at Omar.

Kareem's earlier reluctant tolerance was beginning to turn into alarm. 'Great God, Sultana! What is this? Have you taken Faddel's dwarf, too?'

'Omar is not a dwarf!' I protested. 'Omar is a eunuch!'

Kareem threw his arms into the air. 'Sultana!' His loud voice and gesticulating arm movements caused Amani's birds to flutter around the room in panic.

Amani screamed, 'Father!'

Omar rushed to help Amani gather the birds and return them to the garden. As soon as the door closed behind them, I attempted to soothe Kareem by explaining the morning's events, and how it came about that an aged and wildly dressed eunuch was now living in our home.

When Kareem began to comprehend that not only had I disobeyed his earlier instructions by returning to Faddel's palace, but had created yet another upheaval at that palace while on a second mission of mercy, his tolerance for my behaviour vanished.

Kareem shouted, 'Save me, Allah, from lying lips and deceiving tongues!' The raised veins on his face and neck were alarming.

I tried to tell Kareem about the plight of the poor women being held against their will, but Kareem's loud cries overwhelmed my words. We quickly became involved in a senseless shouting match and our argument ceased only when our voices grew hoarse.

When he fell silent, I tried to tell Kareem the tragic story of the young women held in sexual bondage by Faddel, but even the grim reality of innocent girls imprisoned in a harem made no impact on his anger.

I added meekly, 'I know that I should have first confided in you, husband. But, you already were so burdened with Amani and those birds, that I hesitated.' I leaned close and placed my hand on Kareem's leg. 'Had I not gone with Maha, and made an effort to free those young women, she would never have forgiven me.'

Kareem shook his head angrily. 'What good did you do, Sultana? The women still belong to Faddel. Nothing can change that fact! You well know that no-one in this country will take up the cause of women in such a situation!' He gestured towards the spot where Omar sat previously. 'So, what did you accomplish? The addition of an ancient eunuch to a household that has no need for one!'

Kareem and I were startled to hear Omar clear his throat behind us. From the heaviness now reflected on his sagging face, it was clear that he had overheard Kareem's callous remarks.

'I will leave your home at once, master,' Omar

stuttered in a high, meek tone of voice. 'You are right. A eunuch is a pointless creature. At least these days.'

Omar's eyes were glistening, and I feared that the poor man was going to fall to his knees and burst into tears.

There are times that Kareem can be a sensitive man, and this was one of those times. 'I am sorry for my careless words, Omar. No man is pointless in the eyes of Allah. And, if Faddel does not protest your absence, you are most welcome to live with us.'

Omar's countenance brightened immediately. 'Oh, master, my presence will not be missed in that place! I once left to travel with a visitor from Taif and was away for four months. Upon my return, it was clear that my absence had passed unnoticed by Master Faddel and his wife.'

Omar went on ruefully, 'I was told by other servants that Faddel and Khalidah expressed the hope that I had crept into the bushes and died. Those two even begrudged me what little food my small body requires!' He stroked the fabric of his brocade trousers. 'Master Faddel refused funds for me to purchase more appropriate garments. That is why I wear such ancient attire from the days of my past, master.'

Kareem smiled kindly. 'Here you are welcome to all the food you can eat, Omar. And, I will tell Mohammed to assist you with new clothing. If you are to live with us, then you will dress appropriately.'

Omar looked at me with bright shining eyes before turning back to Kareem. 'Master, God has answered my prayers! I knew that a good woman such as your wife would be paired with a kindly man!'

I glanced at Kareem, thinking that he might join in Omar's praise, but he did not. Instead, he patted Omar on the back. 'Friend, one thing only, do not refer to me as "Master". No man is the master of another. Please call me Prince Kareem.'

Omar nodded. 'It is a long habit that will be hard to break, but I shall try, Prince Kareem.'

With a smile on his face, Kareem then leaned back in the sofa and called out for the servants to bring us tea.

I was astonished to see that my husband's tremendous wrath had been so quickly appeased by this little man! As I thought back, I remembered how Omar had comforted me the previous day, and I realized that this eunuch possessed an enormously calming influence. I looked at Omar with a new thought in mind. Would this little man prove to be an unexpected gift to my overwrought, highly emotional family?

Kareem looked at Omar with kindness. 'Omar, tell us something of your past. I was certain that the last eunuch in Saudi Arabia had died some years ago.'

Omar became animated. 'It would be my great pleasure to tell you anything you ask,' he said with great excitement.

I smiled. I had already noticed that Omar loved to tell stories.

With a genial ease of manners, Omar pulled himself upright, and carefully arranging his full-cut trousers, sat cross-legged on the sofa. When he lifted his head to look at Kareem, his eyes took on a faraway look as he began to relate details of the life he had lived.

'I remember little of *bilad as-Sudan*, known as the "land of the black peoples", but I do know that my family's tribe, the *Humr*, were nomadic cattlemen. We followed the rains and the tall grasses.

'Those were dangerous days. Many African chiefs worked closely with Muslim slave traders, capturing and selling their own people. Every *Humr* mother was burdened with the worry that her children would be stolen from her. Even now, I remember the soft brown eyes of my mother as she looked at me, and her stern warning that I was not to stray far from members of the tribe.' Omar's sad eyes mirrored his own pain. 'I was young and foolish, and failed to obey my mother.

'It was the aim of every young *Humr* male to be praised as a hunter. Small boys were always gathering stones to toss at birds or small animals. I was no different, and one day while gathering smooth stones, I foolishly wandered some distance from the tribe. Just as I was about to toss a stone at a bustard, I was suddenly grabbed from behind and taken away from that place. I never saw my mother again.'

Even after all these years, Omar brushed away tears at the thought of his mother. 'But, that was a long, long time ago.'

Stillness hung in the air. I felt unbelievably sad for the young boy who had been taken from his mother, and for the man who had no chance to experience the life he had been born to live.

Omar began to talk in a low voice, not looking at Kareem or me. 'I was not alone in my misery.

Many men, women and children had been taken from their villages or tribes. We were tied together and led across the land towards the Red Sea. We spent many days and nights travelling. When we finally arrived at the Red Sea, an Egyptian Christian met with our leader. There was low talk concerning the young male captives. Panic ran down the line of captured slaves when the man was overheard saying that a certain number of the youngest boys were to be relieved of their three precious gifts. Unsure of what these precious gifts were, I did not protest too loudly when I was pulled from the line and taken a short distance away from the other captured slaves.'

Plainly uncomfortable, Kareem interrupted Omar. 'One moment, Omar.' He turned to me. 'Sultana, please go to the kitchen and ask the cook to prepare some refreshments.'

I knew Kareem's intention. He did not want me in the room when Omar detailed the graphic tale of his castration. In our conservative Saudi society, my presence would be improper. This, even though Omar was not really considered a man. Poor Omar lived a sad and uncertain fate. He was neither man nor woman, although his status was slightly lower than a man's but higher than a woman's.

I did not object to Kareem's suggestion, although I had already braced myself to hear the lurid details of Omar's castration. I knew that once we were alone, Kareem would willingly tell me everything. But I was too impatient to wait. I decided to listen to the rest of Omar's story from the other side of the door.

'Yes, of course,' I replied, standing up and

leaving the room. I hurried to the kitchen and requested the cook to prepare a selection of refreshments consisting of cheeses, fruits and choice sweets.

Once I left the kitchen, I stepped quietly behind the door leading into the sitting room.

Omar was still speaking, and I soon realized that I had not missed the main part of his story. '. . . man was well-prepared for his duty. His razor was sharp, and without knowing what was about to happen, I was suddenly relieved of my three manly items.'

Kareem gasped loudly, 'Surely, Allah's word was mocked by those men and their cruel actions!'

'Allah was nowhere to be found on that day,' Omar said wistfully, 'although His name was invoked more than once by every boy subjected to this cruel treatment.'

I heard Kareem take a deep breath.

Omar remembered every detail of his ordeal. 'A tube was inserted into the opening that was left in the place of my penis so that the hole would not close. I was bleeding badly, but the bleeding stopped when that man's assistant poured boiling oil on my wounds.' Omar chuckled. 'He presented me with my genitals in a jar, even as I lay writhing in pain! I kept that jar and its contents for many years, until fifteen years ago it was stolen by a cruel prankster.'

'It is a wonder that you did not perish in the midst of all this cruelty,' Kareem managed to say.

'I survived, as you see. A total of ten boys were castrated that day. One died immediately. The rest of us were buried up to our necks in the sand.' He chuckled humourlessly once more. 'Who knows what cruel fool decided that hot sand was a remedy for survival? So, for three days and nights we were given no water or food. At the end, only three of the nine were still among the living.'

As I listened, my knees became weak. This was the most horrid story I had ever heard! Although I knew that in the past eunuchs were prized in many countries, I had never considered the terrible agony those poor men had undergone. I sincerely hoped that God had reserved the hottest places in hell for the vile men who had committed such acts!

Poor Omar continued with his tragic saga. 'Congratulations went all around when the Christian pulled the tube from my small passageway that remained for water, and liquid spurted out; for those men knew that whoever passed water would survive. Only two of the three still living were able to urinate, myself and one other boy. The third boy's hapless body was poisoned by his own urine, and he soon died a tortured, screaming death.

'After the fourth day, we were packed into a ship that set sail for a slave emporium in Constantinople. I had survived castration and the slave trader knew that I would bring a large sum of money.'

I nodded. In those days, eunuchs were prized as trustworthy guards for Muslim women. Only impotent men were allowed in the women's quarters.

Omar's words interrupted my thoughts. 'Therefore, the slave trader treated us two castrated boys more kindly than the other slaves. We were housed on the top deck and fed good food, while those other poor souls kept below were stacked on top of one another during the sea journey. As far as I could tell, they received no food or water. Many were dead by the time we arrived at the harbour of Constantinople.'

I judged that Omar's story had now passed the point that Kareem would object to my hearing, so I returned quietly to the room and sat down.

'Go on,' Kareem said to Omar's questioning eyes. 'It is all right now.'

Omar looked at me and smiled. 'I already told the mistress that I was purchased by a wealthy Turkish man. He owned a number of slaves, but only two eunuchs, and both were growing old. I was told that when I grew tall and strong, I would be the one to guard his women.

'Meanwhile, I was taken by my new master on the pilgrimage to Makkah. My master died there while worshipping at the big mosque, and I became a property of the Makkah authorities. Those men gave me to the grandfather of Faddel, who was owed a favour by the authorities in that city.

'My time with that family was not unhappy. My food was the family's food. At fourteen years of age, I was entrusted to guard the master's wives and female slaves. Time flowed smoothly until after the deaths of Faddel's grandfather *and* father. I had nowhere else to live, so I remained with Faddel.' Omar looked me full in the face. 'Faddel is nothing like his grandfather or his father, mistress.' He paused. 'For someone to answer to Faddel is to be sent to hell and be punished everlastingly.'

I sighed in despair as I suddenly remembered the young women who now belonged to Faddel. Could hell be worse than what those women now endured? Thinking about Faddel, I was reminded of his wife, Khalidah. She could help those young women, if she so chose. I spoke heatedly, 'To my eyes, Khalidah is as wicked as Faddel!'

Omar shrugged his thin shoulders. 'If the master of the house beats a tambourine, do not condemn his family for dancing.'

Kareem looked at me and smiled.

With an instinct that came from being married for many years, I knew that Kareem often wished that I would dance to his tune!

'Never will that happen, husband,' I whispered.

Kareem laughed aloud before turning his attention back to Omar.

Omar straightened his turban as he smiled at Kareem. 'But today, I am more happy than I have been in many years. It is good to live with a kind family.'

Just then several female servants entered the room with refreshments. Omar's eyes twinkled at the sight of the food, and his fingers reached eagerly for the honeyed sweets.

Kareem and I watched in astonishment as Omar quickly consumed more food than could be expected from a man twice his size.

Later that evening, once we were alone in our private quarters, Kareem confessed that he had given much thought to Omar. He tried to convince me that Omar should not live in Arabia, but instead, should be sent to live in one of our palaces abroad. For Omar's safety, no-one in our country could know that the eunuch who had once belonged to Faddel's family had taken refuge with us.

Even though Omar was legally free, and Faddel had previously expressed irritation at housing and feeding an elderly eunuch, he was certain to be insulted that Omar preferred to live with another family. And, who could guess whether Faddel would attempt to take revenge on poor Omar?

At first I was dismayed at the idea of sending poor Omar away. He appeared so pleased and happy with our family. Besides, I adored the little man, and anticipated that his gentle presence might help to bring welcome peace into our family life. After a night of consideration, though, the thought of Omar living the life of a free man in the world outside of Saudi Arabia brought a smile of satisfaction to my face. Besides, we would still see him abroad, I reasoned.

The following morning, Kareem spent some time alone with Omar. The decision was made that Omar would live at our villa in Egypt. In that highly populated country – teeming with Egyptians, Arabs and Africans – a small black man with a high-pitched voice would not be so conspicuous. And the monthly allowance Kareem offered would provide Omar with a personal financial freedom that he had never known.

Omar appeared overjoyed to be returning to the continent where he had been born, and spoke excitedly of taking a trip into Sudan, to locate any remaining members of his family or tribe.

The happiness Kareem and I felt at seeing Omar's joy brought pleasure and contentment. Even Kareem had to agree that some good had come from my second trip to Faddel's palace. While my visit had not benefited the young girls, the eunuch Omar would now live out his life in a wonderful way that he had never dreamed possible!

By the time Omar left for Egypt, we had grown to love him. That little man had quickly become the trusted confidant of every family member. To my astonishment, even Amani cried as she promised Omar that she would remember all that he had told her, and that she would try her best to become a more forgiving and gentle Muslim than she had been.

Each of us greatly looked forward to the day when we could see Omar's kindly face once more.

Prophet Mohammed Defamed

Several days after Omar had departed Saudi Arabia for Egypt, Kareem told me that he and Asad must travel to New York City. Important business matters needed their attention. Knowing that I was still grieving over the plight of the young women in Faddel's harem, Kareem thought that I needed some new experiences to occupy my mind and suggested that I accompany him.

At first I was not anxious to leave, and I was insulted that Kareem did not seem to trust me to remain alone in Saudi Arabia. If my husband believed that I might renew my efforts to obtain those young women's release once he had left the country, he was wrong. Nothing I could say or do could convince Kareem that I was resigned to the hopelessness of the situation. Although I desperately wanted to help those girls, I am not totally devoid of common sense. I fully understood that, when dealing with young girls who had been sold by their own parents and now lived in a country where the government sees no wrong in such a situation, I was, indeed, helpless to resolve the problem.

When I learned that Sara, along with two of our

cousins, Maysa and Huda, were going on the trip to New York, I changed my mind and became eager to accompany them.

Since school had reopened after the Ramadan holiday, Sara and I agreed that our children would remain behind in Riyadh with our eldest sister Nura.

When the day came for us to depart, our party flew on one of our private jets to London. After a brief stopover in that city, we continued on with our journey to the United States.

Including the three maids who were accompanying us – Afaaf, Libby and Betty – there were seven women on the plane. To pass the time, we began to entertain each other with amusing stories, but our laughter ceased when Maysa changed the tone by sharing one particular story that we found horrifying.

Maysa is a Palestinian who is married to Naif Al Sa'ud, one of my favourite cousins. Although lively and attractive, Maysa could not be called beautiful, but she is highly popular with everyone who meets her. As a child born in Hebron, in occupied Palestine, Maysa's childhood had been full of incident. Over the years, our family had heard many stories from Maysa about fleeing refugees, street battles with Israeli soldiers, and her younger brothers' participation in the more recent intifada, the Palestinian uprising against the Israelis.

The Palestinian Arabs have always been more attuned to women's rights than have the desert Arabs. Recognizing Maysa's intelligence, her parents made many sacrifices so that their daughter could be educated. Maysa was sent to Beirut to be schooled at the prestigious American University of Beirut. It was there that she met my cousin Naif. The vivacious Maysa easily captured Naif's heart. Deeply in love when they married, they enjoy a happier union than most married couples in my land. Although Maysa and Naif have only one child, a daughter, Naif has never indicated the slightest interest in taking a second wife for the purpose of enlarging his family.

Maysa is a caring person who always concerns herself with the problems of others. If she is not worried about the starving babies in embargoed Iraq, she is thinking about earthquake victims in Iran or in China.

A few weeks previous to our trip, Maysa had returned from her annual visit with her Palestinian family in the Arab city of Hebron. While on that visit, Maysa had witnessed the most heinous sight imaginable to the eyes of a Muslim.

Maysa's voice now quivered as she related what she had seen. 'I knew that day we should not have gone out! There had been unrest for several weeks, and I did not want to take a chance that my dear mother might be struck by a wayward stone. But Mother was restless, and insisted that we would walk only to the corner of our street, and then back. We wanted only a breath of fresh air, nothing more!

'By the time we arrived at the end of our street, we were relieved to see that all was quiet. So, we decided to walk one street further.' Maysa slapped her forehead with her hand. '*That* was our mistake!'

Maysa became agitated at the very memory.

'We saw a young woman running ahead of

us, nailing posters to the walls. We thought the woman was a brave Palestinian demonstrator putting up signs of protest against the Israelis!'

Maysa slapped her forehead once more, only harder this time. 'How were two naïve women to know that this woman was a Zionist attacking our beloved Prophet!'

She slumped back into her seat and moaned at the memory.

Sara patted her gently. 'Do not tell us, Maysa, if it is so painful for you.'

Maysa sat up straight. 'I *must* tell you, Sara! Every Muslim should know this story!' Maysa is a religious woman, but not so strict as to be annoying.

Every passenger on the plane, including Asad and Kareem, was listening.

'Well, I tell you, I have never had such a shock. Our curiosity aroused, Mother and I stopped in front of one of those posters. It took us some moments to comprehend that what the poster depicted was a likeness no Muslim should ever live to see.'

She stared vacantly ahead, sitting in silence until Sara touched her arm. 'Maysa?'

'I tell you, Sara. My own lips hesitate to say the words.'

I spoke up. 'For God's sake, Maysa! Tell us! The suspense is driving us mad!'

Maysa's face became pale as she looked intently into the face of each of us in turn. Her voice lowered to a whisper. 'It was a caricature of our Prophet.' She buried her face in her hands before crying out, 'On that poster, our beloved Prophet Mohammed was shown to be a pig!'

Every woman on the plane gasped in horror.

I struggled to keep my composure as I clasped Kareem's hand tightly.

'Yes! There it was, right before my eyes! The Prophet Mohammed depicted as a pig! I tell you, my heart nearly stopped. And, Mother? Well, she swooned! I had to call for help to carry her back to our apartment! She has still not recovered! She is no longer the person she once was!'

Poor Maysa collapsed against the back of her seat. 'Since that time, I have suffered horrible nightmares. Each night the Prophet Mohammed comes to visit me in a dream. In that dream the Prophet has the body of a man and the disgusting face of a pig!'

'Oh, Maysa,' Sara murmured with sympathy. 'How terrible for you.'

Dreams of our beloved Prophet as a pig! I drew back, regretting that Sara had invited Maysa to come with us on the trip. I, for one, did not want to be contaminated by being near to a person with such wicked dreams!

Maysa began to weep in earnest. 'I tell you, Sara, it is getting so that I fear to close my eyes, for I am surely committing the most vile sin because I cannot prevent this dream.'

I began to feel remorse at my initial reaction, and tried to look more kindly on Maysa.

Libby, my Filipino maid, said, 'I recently read a newspaper article which claimed that enemies of Arab countries were coating their bullets with pig lard to use against Muslims in war.'

This was a well-known scandal. Should a Muslim soldier be wounded or killed by such tainted ammunition, that soldier would be automatically excluded from paradise. The Islamic religion does not allow Muslims to make any contact with pig flesh. A Muslim believes that merely touching the flesh of a pig would keep him or her from entering paradise.

Maysa's muffled sobs grew louder, and she pleaded with Sara to pinch her if she must – anything to keep her from falling asleep and dreaming her blasphemous dream.

I prayed to God that He would eradicate that evil image from Maysa's mind. Shaking my head in sadness, I turned around and began walking towards my seat. Just as I was sitting down, I noticed that Sara's maid, Afaaf, was sitting alone and weeping. I motioned to Sara and together we approached Afaaf.

Sara touched Afaaf's shoulder. 'Afaaf, are you unwell, dear?'

Afaaf's face was a picture of complete misery. She tried to speak, but could not. Finally, after Libby brought her a glass of water and encouraged her to take a few sips, Afaaf told us, 'I am sorry to cry, but this terrible story reminded me of how our Holy Prophet has been defamed, and in so many ways . . .' Afaaf began weeping again. '. . . and His name and His holy words are often used as a weapon of revenge and evil, even by His own people. Does that not besmirch our Prophet, also?'

Sara nodded, but did not speak.

I stood helpless as poor Afaaf sobbed. If there was anyone in the world who had a reason to cry, it was Afaaf.

Afaaf was a refugee from Afghanistan. Although she had escaped the war in her country, she could never recover from the terrible losses she had suffered. Afaaf had lost her entire family. Her parents and one brother had been killed in the long war that preceded the brutal Taliban regime's coming to power. Afaaf and her younger sister were left alone, without any male protection in a country now ruled by men who were determined to totally control every aspect of a woman's life.

In 1994, when the Taliban adherents who now rule Afghanistan came to power, they had carried the suppression of women to a new level. While the lives of Saudi women can be unbelievably bleak, I had learned from Afaaf that the lives of women in Afghanistan were much more tragically harsh than our own.

In the Taliban's drive to restore Islamic purity, they had launched a horrifying assault on their own women. Not only were Afghan women forced to cover their bodies and faces in the *burqa*, a thick, tent-like garment even more awkward and uncomfortable than the Saudi *abaaya* and veil, but women were also forbidden to even talk loudly or to laugh in public. Even though women were totally hidden by the *burqa*, the men in power claimed that the sound of women's voices alone had the power to excite men! Additionally, women were banned from going to school, from wearing make-up, jewelry or high-heeled shoes, and even from working to feed themselves and their families. Afghan women were banned from every activity of normal life.

The harsh regime's edicts extended even to small children. In Afghanistan it was now a crime to watch television and videos, play with toys and games, listen to music, or even to read books!

When the Taliban came to power, Afaaf's own

life changed dramatically. She had once been a teacher, but she was no longer allowed to teach. She had once worn her hair in a short style, but had been told that it was a crime for a woman to cut her hair!

Shortly after the Taliban gained power, Afaaf's sister had been caught speaking to a man to whom she was not related. She had been merely asking this former neighbour about his elderly parents. A group of teenage boys saw this exchange and demanded to see proof that Afaaf's sister was a relative to the man. Of course, no such proof was possible, and she had been taken before the Department to Protect Virtue and Prevent Vice, where she was condemned by a panel of male judges to receive fifty lashes.

Afaaf had been forced to witness her beloved sister being tied to a pole and lashed with a leather strap. She had nursed her wounded sibling back to health, but the poor woman was so aggrieved at the turn her life had taken that she swallowed a large amount of rat poison. Since women were banned from hospitals, she had died in Afaaf's arms.

Having nothing more to lose, Afaaf fled to the Pakistani border. After slipping into Pakistan, she had been employed by one of Asad's men, who happened to be in Pakistan to search for domestic staff to work in Saudi Arabia.

Afaaf put her face in her hands and sighed deeply. 'Fanatical Muslim men defame the Prophet and his words in their determination to destroy every woman's life.'

I was so struck with sadness that I felt like crying along with the poor woman. For me, the unfortunate Afaaf was one of the saddest human beings I had ever known. She was truly alone in the world – and all because of evil men who intentionally twist the meaning of the words of the Holy Prophet in their obsession to control women.

I slowly walked to a window seat and sat down. I pressed my head against the small windowpane. After covering myself with a blanket, I closed my eyes. I felt a rush of gladness that I lived in Saudi Arabia rather than Afghanistan. I almost laughed at the irony of such an idea, for there is much danger for women in Saudi Arabia, where fanatical men have the powerful capability to ruin lives, too.

The year before, an appalling event occurred which again came to my mind. A young woman by the name of Hussah, who was one of Maha's friends at school, had discovered the enormous power wielded by men over women in the name of religion.

Hussah was an unusually pretty girl with a charming disposition. Her school grades proved her intelligence, and her bubbly personality gained her many friends. Maha often reported that Hussah enlivened dull school days.

Hussah had visited our palace on more than one occasion, and I, too, grew fond of this young woman. My affection for her increased when I learned that her own mother had died the previous year, and that her father's new wife disliked Hussah. Despite this sadness, Hussah was always smiling and friendly.

When Hussah had been three years old, her family moved to Egypt where they remained for ten years. In Egypt, Hussah had grown accustomed to more independence than girls are allowed in the inflexible atmosphere of Saudi Arabia. When the family returned to Riyadh, despite her early years of freedom in Egypt, Hussah had accepted Saudi life without complaint. She obediently wore the veil and *abaaya* in public places, and did not complain about the other restrictions imposed on women.

Inside the safe confines of her family's compound, Hussah was a normal modern girl. She wore jeans and T-shirts, she chatted for long hours on the telephone, and she spent many hours swimming in the family pool. Hussah had always enjoyed sports activities, and was sad that women in Saudi Arabia are not allowed to compete in events such as the Olympics. Such a dream is unattainable for Saudi females, so Hussah's swimming achievements had to remain for her pleasure only.

Hussah's tragic fate was caused by her love of swimming. Hussah often wore bikinis when swimming her daily laps, and these costumes displayed the fact that Hussah had been blessed with a voluptuous body.

Unfortunately for Hussah, the family living next door to her home were Islamic fundamentalists. When the eldest son of that family caught a glimpse of the sexy Hussah in her skimpy swimsuit, her life was for ever changed.

Although high walls surround every Saudi home, the higher storeyed home will often have a view of adjacent gardens. Hussah's family home was a one-storey villa, while the neighbour's home reached three storeys. If someone on the third floor should happen to glance out of a certain small window, he or she was rewarded with a view of the bordering garden and swimming pool. While most considerate Muslim neighbours will seal up such a window, this was not the case here.

This young man, Fadi, was studying to become a *mutawwa*. After observing Hussah in her swimsuit, he became so incensed that he purchased a long-lens camera and took many photographs of the young woman as she swam in the privacy of her own pool. As fate would have it, on one of the days Fadi was secretly taking photographs, Hussah's bikini top accidentally loosened. Her full breasts were exposed only long enough for the neighbour to capture that image on film.

Filled with the venom that only the self-righteous possess, Fadi complained to the local religious authorities that Hussah was a wicked sinner who had *intentionally* exposed her breasts to him. In his fervour, he falsely claimed that Hussah's eyes had met his, and that she had smiled invitingly just before lowering her swimming costume. He further declared that Hussah's act had caused him to sin by dreaming of naked vixens. In order to recover his former state of purity, he demanded that Hussah be stoned to death!

If the local authorities had agreed with Fadi, the poor girl would be in her grave. But her father was pressured to believe that the years spent abroad and the small freedoms his daughter had once enjoyed had influenced Hussah to become a flagrant exhibitionist. These men of religion who talked with him believed that education and hobbies for women would ensure the decay of Saudi society.

They generously agreed not to punish Hussah, if her father himself would take certain harsh measures. Hussah was to be removed from school, she was to be forbidden to swim, and most importantly, she should be married within the month. They also insisted that Hussah's husband should be an older man practised in controlling wayward females. In fact, these men even had such a husband in mind. They believed that Fadi's own father would be a good choice, as he already had three wives, and they knew him to be a strict and pious man. He would not allow Hussah opportunities that might bring shame on her family name. Fortunately for Hussah, they reported, this neighbour had seen Hussah's photograph and had agreed to accept the moral duty of 'subduing' this wicked seducer!

No mention was made of the fact that Fadi was obviously a voyeur or he would have had the decency to turn his eyes away from another man's private garden. Nor was it acknowledged that the sight of Hussah's picture might have aroused sexual desire, rather than religious obligation, in Fadi's father.

At first, Hussah's father fought for his daughter. But, he was outnumbered. His new wife sided with the *mutawwas*, claiming that Hussah was not the pure daughter he believed, and that the girl was sure to ruin the family name with her embarrassing behaviour. Overwhelmed by pressure from all fronts, and believing that an even greater punishment would be inflicted on his daughter if he did not submit to the religious authorities, Hussah's father finally agreed to the marriage.

In a moment, Hussah's life had gone from

relative freedom to the greatest oppression. After a quick wedding, Hussah had managed to telephone Maha only once, but the sound of her shaky voice was cut short when the line was abruptly disconnected.

With the stories of these two women's utterly ruined lives uppermost in my mind, I questioned how it was that so many men of the Islamic faith failed to remember that Prophet Mohammed never tired of praising the infinite mercy of Allah? Every chapter of the Koran, except one, begins with the *bismillah*, 'In the name of God the Compassionate, the Merciful.'

The sad truth was that Afaaf was right. A large number of Muslim men *do* defame the Prophet and his teachings when they oppress women in his name.

And, what can we women do? In the Muslim world, it is believed that only men may interpret the Koran. If any woman complained of the way women such as Afaaf or Hussah were treated, she would be accused of attacking our faith – an unforgivable crime assuring the severest punishment.

These thoughts were interrupted when I heard Maysa, who in spite of all her efforts had nodded off in her seat, cry out in her sleep. Knowing that the unfortunate Maysa was at that moment witnessing our beloved Prophet as a pig, I knew that her dreams were even more disturbing than my own thoughts. I would not be in Maysa's situation for all the freedom in the world.

Stolen Angels

Our plane soon landed at the La Guardia airport in New York. Thankfully, we passed through customs and immigration quickly since one of the Saudi officials from our consulate offices in New York was on hand to guide us through and ensure VIP treatment.

Ten limousines stood ready to transport us, and our luggage, to the New York Plaza Hotel. Everyone was excited, so it took long moments for us to decide who would ride with whom, in what car.

Exasperated, Kareem began to shout, telling us that we reminded him of large black birds flitting from one place to another. The other women calmed down and quickly found a place to sit, but I stood aside, and stubbornly refused to enter the limousine until Kareem apologized for his rude remarks.

Kareem saw that I was willing to take a firm stand, so he lifted his shoulders in resignation and said, 'I am sorry, Sultana. Now, *please*, get in the car!'

Somewhat appeased, I sat with Sara and Maysa. I watched as the limousine driver rolled his eyes; obviously, he was unaccustomed to the histrionic displays of female Saudi royalty. Despite the disruptions, we were soon on our way to the Plaza Hotel.

Kareem had reserved an entire wing of the grand old hotel that had long been our favourite during our visits to New York City. Time and again, the staff at the Plaza had proven their discretion in providing hospitality to guests from wealthy Middle Eastern countries. Such thoughtful service is not forgotten.

As we drove into the city, I watched with delight as women drivers sped past us. I never tire of such a sight when I visit other lands! Women are not allowed to drive in Saudi Arabia, and since this restriction has no basis in our religion, it has always angered me. Years ago, Kareem took me for driving lessons in the desert. I learned to drive, but I have never driven through the streets of my own country. To add insult to injury, a woman of forty years is forbidden to drive in Saudi Arabia, yet boys no more than eight or nine years old are frequently seen at the wheel of a speeding car filled with terrified women. Some Bedouin men in my country give their camels better treatment than they do their wives. In Saudi Arabia, it is not an uncommon sight to see baby camels riding in the passenger seat of an air-conditioned truck while veiled women are riding in the open back!

Now, watching American women drive confidently through the city traffic lifted my spirits. Surely, while visiting such a country as the United States, I could finally forget about the misfortunes that plague so many females. I could take immediate pleasure in the freedom for women that I saw all around me. Unfortunately, as happens so frequently in my life, my wish was *not* to be granted.

The traffic was not heavy, and our automobile ride from the airport to the hotel lasted no more than thirty-five minutes. A second consulate employee had ensured special security arrangements upon our arrival at the hotel, so we were all escorted directly to our rooms.

We women parted company in the hotel corridor. In a high state of excitement, we agreed we would not give in to jet lag, but would dress as quickly as possible, and then meet in Sara's suite before setting off for our long-awaited shopping spree.

Once Kareem and I had inspected our suite and found it to our satisfaction, he turned to me with a smile, and said, 'Sultana, I must leave soon, but before I leave, I want to give you a small gift.'

I stared at Kareem in wonder. What now? My husband is a generous man who often showers me with expensive gifts at the most unexpected times.

He then slipped a platinum American Express credit card into my hand. 'Sultana, you can use this card to purchase anything you wish up to five hundred thousand in American dollars.'

He smiled at the expression on my face. 'Darling, you have been under such a strain, lately. You deserve to have a good time. But', he added, 'this card will probably not be enough to cover jewelry. Should you find something special you want, just ask the manager to hold it, and I will send one of my bankers tomorrow to complete the purchase.'

I turned the card over in my hands. This would be the first time I had ever been given one. When I shop in Saudi Arabia, I never pay for my own purchases. In fact, I rarely know the price of the items I purchase. I always leave the details regarding payment to one of our business managers. I am accustomed to merely pointing out what I want, knowing that the items will be paid for later. Today, though, I felt pleased that we were not accompanied by one of our business managers and that I would be responsible for charging my own purchases.

Kareem then retrieved a large bundle of American currency of various denominations out of his briefcase and literally stuffed my handbag. Three times he cautioned me not to let strangers see that money; he did not want New York muggers smashing in my head.

Just then Asad knocked at the door, and Kareem rushed out with his brother to attend a business meeting.

I was left alone at last. I telephoned Libby and asked her to come to my room and prepare my bath. After the long plane ride, I needed to freshen up. Later, as I soaked in my bath, I lazily decided that I would shop at Bergdorf Goodman, a favourite department store for many Al Sa'ud women.

Once I was dressed, I joined the other women waiting in Sara's suite. After lengthy discussions, we decided that Sara and Maysa would accompany me to Bergdorf Goodman. Libby, Betty and Afaaf stood silently, waiting for our instructions. Generally we take our servants with us when we go out shopping, but on this day our hearts were so sad for Afaaf that Sara and I decided to surprise them with a cash bonus and the day off. All three women smiled gratefully before leaving to shop on Fifth Avenue.

The seventh woman in our party, Cousin Huda, declined to join us. For her, shopping could wait. Instead, she announced, she planned to remain in her suite and indulge herself in fine food and drink. In fact, she had ordered three large tins of Beluga caviar already, and was now looking forward to an afternoon spent eating caviar, drinking champagne and watching American soap operas on television.

I stared in amazement at Huda. Why would any woman choose to remain locked in a hotel suite to *eat* instead of shopping in New York City? We Saudi women remain secluded for so much of our lives that one would think such an opportunity as this would not be missed.

I shrugged but said nothing to convince Huda otherwise. She was not one of my favourite cousins, and we did not have a particularly close relationship. I could not understand her obsession with food, and every conversation with her involved hearing about some special dish or another that she had either prepared or eaten. One story that was repeated in our family with great amusement was that Huda and her husband often flew to France for a single meal.

Only Sara was kind enough to endure her long conversations describing gourmet dishes. For this reason, Huda had attached herself to Sara, and my gentle sister was too kind to pull away. So I was relieved that Huda was staying behind.

Our walk to Bergdorf Goodman took only minutes, but for me, it was an exhilarating walk, for I never tire of such simple freedoms taken for granted by most of the women of the world. Here I was, in broad daylight, dressed in a form-fitting blue Armani jacket and skirt, walking down a city street crowded with men. Here, women need not fear the sudden appearance of the *mutawwa*, the Saudi religious police, with their sticks to strike any woman immoral enough to dress in such provocative attire.

I felt a great gaiety, and not a little vanity. I have always been sad that I was not blessed with long limbs, as are my sisters. Yet my legs, although short, are shapely. I was well aware that my matching blue high-heeled shoes displayed my legs to a good advantage. A breeze blew through my long wavy hair, which I deliberately tossed as I chatted with Sara and Maysa. I felt exuberant and happy to have the freedom to show my face, display my lovely clothes, and walk the streets of a large city – and all without a hovering male escort!

I thought that Western women are indeed more fortunate than they realize. This thought led me to Afaaf. I knew that she must be enjoying this sweet day of freedom even more than me.

I glanced at Maysa and smiled. She had not taken particular care with her personal appearance. Yet, an expensive black suit covers many flaws. Sara was dressed more demurely than Maysa or me, in a modest cream-coloured silk dress with a high neck and long sleeves, but as always she looked stunning.

I felt deliciously feminine and pretty when I became aware of several men staring at us as we walked down the street. While my flamboyance drew their initial attention, I noticed that their eyes lingered longest on Sara, who, of course, completely failed to notice that we were the focus of so many appreciative glances.

Once we entered the department store, I followed my usual behaviour when confronted with such a dazzling display of merchandise: I purchased every item that caught my eye! In a short time I had selected fifteen expensive evening gowns to wear to parties and weddings. There is much competition among us Al Sa'ud women, so I shopped for the newest and most original styles. I did not take the time to try on these dresses. My custom is to buy many, many clothes, and then give away what does not fit or I do not like.

I was not totally selfish, though; I also found many wonderful gifts for my children and Kareem.

When I informed a clerk that I would take a dozen silk blouses in one style and colour, she quickly established that we were members of the royal family of Saudi Arabia, and called one of the store managers. After that, we were accompanied by the manager as we examined Bergdorf Goodman's huge collection of designer wear.

Soon, more than ten employees had been summoned to carry our heavy shopping bags. It was evident in the faces around us that our spending spree at Bergdorf Goodman's was a most exciting event.

Although Sara and Maysa's purchases together filled no more than five shopping bags, I required more than thirty bags for the items I had selected. Surely, I thought, Kareem would need to replenish my special card with additional funds; I was astonished when the manager said that my total expenditure at Bergdorf Goodman's amounted to only $388,000.

Sara was not surprised when I told her of Kareem's gift, as most members of our family are fabulously wealthy and on our shopping trips we buy anything we desire. Still, our purchases are trifling compared to the real estate and business deals our husbands were conducting even as we shopped.

Maysa had been born into a Palestinian family of modest means, so her reaction was one of disapproval at my extravagance. I overheard her when she murmured, 'Multiply your possessions, increase your burdens.' Maysa looked at me and shook her head sadly. 'If Allah chooses to bless me with an additional hundred years of life, I will never adjust to the reckless spending that goes on in this family. Really, Sultana, surely by now even you are wearied of buying endless party dresses and fine jewelry?'

I was not offended by her words. Who could be angry with a woman who lived such an exemplary life of selfless generosity? I knew that Maysa preferred to spend her husband's wealth on the poor. Once I heard that Naif and Maysa supported over eighty Palestinian families living on the West Bank; not only housing, feeding and clothing them, but also paying for the education of the children.

I hugged Maysa just to let her know that she had not angered me. I did not bother to justify my extravagant lifestyle, however, for I felt comfortable in the knowledge that Kareem and I give much more of our wealth to the poor than is required by our faith. What more were we to do?

After we returned from our exhausting shopping adventure, I retired to my suite to rest before dinner.

Kareem had not returned by the late afternoon, and knowing that my sister and the other women in our party were most likely still resting in their rooms, I became restless. I decided to telephone several American women whom I had befriended many years before.

I was pleased to hear the voice of a dear friend, Anne, who, upon hearing my voice, squealed 'Thank God you have called, Sultana! I desperately wanted to call you in Riyadh, but feared someone might overhear our conversation.'

I smiled. Anne is convinced that all telephone lines in my country are tapped.

'Sultana, a terrible thing has happened! A little American girl, not yet five years old, has been kidnapped and taken into your country. Her Saudi father took her from her American mother. The mother is hysterical, of course, and I was hoping that you might help us locate her child.'

My heart sank as I listened to her story. Was I *never* to escape these disturbing stories? Every day of my life I had heard about exploited, ill-treated and abused women, but unlike most other Saudi women, I could not accept that this was merely a woman's lot. And, some years before, I had come to the sad realization that the abuse of women was not unique to Saudi Arabia. This was a worldwide phenomenon.

Sadly, my victories in helping such women were woefully few. And, now, my hopes had been dashed of putting aside such worries and enjoying a few carefree days in America. Already my heart ached for the little girl and her mother.

Knowing that Anne was waiting for my answer,

I took a deep breath. 'Anne, you know that it is difficult to help anyone in this situation in my country.'

With a note of sadness in her voice, Anne said, 'I understand, Sultana, but I was hoping you could do *something*.'

'Is this father a member of my family, the Al Sa'uds?'

'No. He is not royalty.'

'Well, at least tell me what happened.' With a sigh, I glanced at the clock on the bedside table. Dinner would have to wait.

'Whether you can or can't do anything, at least this mother will be pleased when I tell her that I've spoken with you.'

'Tell me all that you know,' I said, as I lit a cigarette and inhaled deeply. This could take some time.

'The mother of this child is a woman by the name of Margaret McClain. She is an instructor at Arkansas State University, and it was there that she met and married a Saudi student named Abdulbaset Al-Omary.'

Al-Omary? I did not personally know a Saudi family by that name. But, as my life revolves around members of the royal family, my lack of knowledge was not surprising.

'From what I have learned, the marriage unravelled rather quickly,' Anne said. 'Once they were legally married, the charming and affectionate suitor quickly changed into a jealous and unreasonable husband.'

'That is not uncommon with Arab men,' I muttered. I had never discovered the reason for this disturbing and consistent pattern of behaviour in many Arab men who woo non-Muslim women. Since inside Saudi Arabia few men meet their wives prior to their arranged marriages, Saudi men have no occasion to be charming before they marry. But, when it comes to romancing women from other countries, no lover could be more charming and attentive than a Saudi suitor, or indeed any Arab nationality including Syrians, Egyptians, Kuwaitis and Jordanians.

Tender words are spoken, gifts are given, and promises are made. Usually, no mention is made of the potential problems of different cultural and religious backgrounds. But, once the woman has been lured into marriage, the man too often turns into a tyrant, becoming abusive and rude to his wife, or becoming too interested in other pretty women.

Differences in religion and culture can soon begin to create serious marital problems. The woman's normal way of dressing, which was greeted with compliments during their courtship, is now declared too revealing. Loud, abusive accusations are thrown into her face if she should dare speak to another man.

What few non-Arabs realize is that *every* Arab man is accustomed to getting his way in all family situations. There will be no peace at home until he is recognized as the undisputed ruler, a fact that many non-Arab wives do not realize until it is too late.

I had seen this over and over, for a number of my cousins married women from Europe and America. These Saudi cousins would profess to love everything about their foreign wives before they were married, but, after marriage, they would suddenly seem to detest everything that they had previously claimed to love.

When the couple begin to have children, the husband will invariably insist that the children be raised solely as Muslims. The mother's religious heritage is considered of no importance.

If divorce results, the woman is in serious danger of losing custody of her children. Islamic law says that mothers may only keep their sons until they are seven, and although daughters may remain with their mothers until puberty, in Muslim countries the age of puberty for females is often as young as eight years old. And, if a Saudi Arabian man should claim custody of his sons or daughters at any age, the mother has no legal recourse. If the children live in another country, Arab fathers often later steal their children and bring them back to their country. Few Arab governments will interfere on the mother's behalf when an Arab man has custody of his own children.

Anne's story interrupted my thoughts. 'Margaret had a daughter, Heidi, by Abdulbaset, but the couple divorced soon after the child's birth.

'Although Abdulbaset often made threats that he would never allow his daughter to be raised in America, he was still attending school in this country. Therefore, temporarily, Heidi was safe. Or so Margaret thought.

'Then, just a few months ago, Abdulbaset took Heidi on his weekend visitation. When the weekend passed, he failed to return his daughter to her mother. The distraught mother has not seen her child since that time. A week or so afterwards, Margaret received a telephone call from

Abdulbaset, and he claimed to have Heidi with him in Saudi Arabia.'

'Poor, poor woman,' I murmured, wondering how any mother could bear such a terrible loss.

Anne's voice lowered. 'Sultana, Heidi is Margaret's youngest child. Her other two children, by her first marriage, are much older than Heidi. The whole family is heartsick at this loss. I have never felt so sorry for anyone in my life.'

'My own heart is breaking at the thought of her misery,' I whispered.

'Isn't there anything that you can do? Poor Margaret can think of nothing else.'

My thoughts were racing. What *could* I do? What help could I possibly offer? Truthfully, I could think of nothing. Finally I asked, 'What about your own government? This woman should take her story to your President.'

Anne laughed. 'Sultana! No ordinary American citizen would be allowed to speak personally to the President about such a thing!'

'Oh?' I answered in surprise. 'In Saudi Arabia, the simplest of men can approach our King. It is not unusual for many small problems involving Saudi citizens to be resolved by the King, himself. Actually, our King regularly travels around the country visiting various tribes so that people can approach him more easily.' How could it be more difficult to see a President than a King?

'No, Sultana. That is not our way here. America is too big. Of course, Margaret has contacted the US State Department. But there is little our government can do when the situation involves another country's sovereignty.'

'I do not understand. An American child has been taken from its mother. Why does your government not intervene in such a situation?'

From what I had seen of American soldiers in Saudi Arabia, I could envision their raiding this Abdulbaset Al-Omary's home and simply returning this child to her mother. What good is a government if it cannot perform a simple act such as returning a child to its mother?

'No . . . no. Apparently, if the child is in Saudi Arabia, it is under Saudi law. It would be up to your government alone to return Heidi.' Anne hesitated. 'But the Saudis will not, of course.'

I feared poor Margaret would never get her child back.

'What do you know of this Abdulbaset Al-Omary?' I asked. 'Where does he work? Where does he live?'

'Well, Margaret has never been to Saudi Arabia, and she has no idea where he lives. He has a degree from Arkansas State University, so he is qualified to teach computer programming. But, since Abdulbaset so recently returned to Saudi Arabia, Margaret has no way of knowing if he has a job.'

'Hmmm.' I was thinking how I might help. If only there were a telephone number or a home address.

'Anne, I cannot rescue this child. You know that. But, if the mother can provide pictures of Heidi and her father, I will do my best to locate her, but don't raise her hopes too much, please.'

'I have a recent picture of Heidi,' Anne said, 'but I will have to telephone Margaret about a picture of the father.'

'His evil act shames every Saudi and every Muslim,' I murmured.

'Well, Margaret says that Abdulbaset professes to be a devout Muslim.'

'Believe me, Anne, no truly good Muslim would steal a child away from its mother,' I said angrily.

Before we ended our conversation, Anne promised to send any additional information on this case to me at the Plaza Hotel.

I sighed deeply, overcome with a depressing vision of the innocent Heidi's bewilderment at finding herself in a strange country, far away from her loving mother. My sorrow soon turned to anger, which grew until I began to feel an unreasoning hatred towards every man.

When Kareem returned to our hotel suite I refused to answer his queries about my day of shopping. Confused by my surliness, he persisted with his questioning until I burst out, 'You, and every other man on earth, should be flogged, Kareem!'

Kareem's mouth dropped in surprise, and his comical expression finally convinced me to tell him the reason for my distress.

'I telephoned Anne.'

Kareem's lips pressed into a thin line. 'Oh?' Although he likes Anne he believes she is a woman who would rather climb a wall than go through an unlocked gate. But I know that Anne's wilfulness is borne of her sincere desire to help many people, and for that I like and admire her.

I told Kareem the details of my conversation with Anne. His reaction was exactly as I would have predicted. Despite the fact that he is more sympathetic to feminist issues than most Arab men, he is reluctant to waste time on problems that he believes are unsolvable.

'Sultana, when will you ever learn that it is *impossible* for one woman to solve *every* other woman's problem?'

'That is why we need help from men – men in power!'

Kareem shook his head in a determined manner. 'I refuse to get involved in this situation, Sultana. This is a personal matter best dealt with by members of the family.'

I could not restrain my urge to strike Kareem for one moment longer! I kicked out at his leg, but missed.

A laughing Kareem grabbed me and held me close.

I broke down in tears. Without the help of our men, how would we women ever change the course of women's lives? Men had all the political power!

In his desire to alter the course of the evening, Kareem began to kiss my face and tell me, 'It's just that I worry about you, Sultana.' He stroked my back. 'You have such small shoulders, darling, yet you try to carry every problem afflicting women on these delicate shoulders.'

I refused to respond.

Kareem studied my face carefully before saying, 'Darling, I have a special gift for you. I was saving it for later, but now seems an appropriate time.'

I resisted Kareem's attempt to kiss my lips. I was not interested in yet another expensive gift.

'It's not what you think, darling.' He paused. 'I wrote a poem for you.'

I leaned back in surprise. We Arabs are 'people

of the ear', rather than 'people of the books', and we are often inclined to express our strongest feelings by composing poetry and reading it aloud.

Yet, Kareem was one of the few Arabs I knew who rarely arranged his thoughts and emotions into poetry. My husband has an analytical mind, which I attribute to his lawyer's training.

Kareem gently led me towards a chair. 'Sit down, darling.'

He knelt on the floor and took my hands into his, his eyes staring straight into mine. His strong, clear voice lowered to a lover's whisper.

You go first.
Go through the door before me.
Enter the limousine while I wait by your side.
Enter the shops while I stand behind, guarding your back.
Sit at the table before me.
Please, sample the tastiest morsels while I sit quietly.
My desire is that you go first, in every occasion of earthly life.
Only once will I go before you,
And that will be at my last moment.
For when death claims us, you must go last.
Because I can't live one second without you.

Kareem kissed my hands.

Overwhelmed with emotion, I couldn't speak. Finally I sputtered, 'Kareem, that's the most beautiful thing you've ever said. The most wonderful gift you could have ever given me, you have just laid at my feet.' I added, 'A basket of diamonds would offer less pleasure.'

Kareem arched his eyebrows in amusement. 'Oh? Be careful what you say, Sultana, or I'll give the basket of diamonds to beggars.'

I smiled.

Kareem stroked my face with his hand. 'Now, Sultana, tell me, did you enjoy your shopping trip?'

I felt a flash of guilt. I am indeed fortunate to have a husband who provides me with my every desire. 'Of course, darling. I had a most wonderful time. I bought many lovely things. No man I know is more generous towards his family.'

My words greatly pleased Kareem.

It is a source of great pride for our Saudi husbands that they are able to acquire anything that their wives and children might covet. There is a heated competition between the Al Sa'ud men as each attempts to surpass the other in buying their families the rarest adornments and the most precious possessions.

But, secretly, the high-priced trinkets that money could buy were no longer bringing Kareem's wife joy or happiness. In the past, I had sought solace for my problems by buying many beautiful and expensive possessions. But something had changed. I realized that spending sprees like mine that morning would no longer provide me with the needed psychological consolation.

What was happening to me? Was I becoming like Maysa? I wondered. Such a change in personality would disrupt everything familiar in our lives. Certainly, Kareem would not know how to react to a woman who had lost her fondness for expensive jewels and beautiful clothes. I did not want a barrier between my husband and me. Eventually I would have to share these strange and new sensibilities with Kareem. But not today. We were both exhausted.

Kareem continued to worry about my lingering depression and, since he was going to be busy with business meetings, he asked Sara to keep a close watch on me for the remainder of the trip.

Sara insisted that we enjoy whatever New York City had to offer, and we did. We saw two Broadway plays; visited the American Museum of Natural History and The Guggenheim Museum; and dined at some of the finest restaurants in the world, Le Bernardin, Le Cirque, Lutece and The Quilted Giraffe.

The day before we were to depart New York City, I received the parcel from my friend Anne. I ripped it open and carefully studied its contents. I was pleased to see that a colour photograph of little Heidi was enclosed. She was a beautiful child with a big smile.

Several typed pages of information were also enclosed, including facts about other young children stolen by Saudi fathers from their American mothers and taken out of the country without permission. I was shocked to learn that over 10,000 children, nearly 2,000 of them American, had been illegally taken from their non-Arab mothers by their Saudi fathers, and were now living in Saudi Arabia.

As I read individual stories of mothers who had not seen their young children for many years, I wept. The pain of losing a child was worse than any other loss; of that, I was certain.

Sifting through the material, I saw a photograph of Heidi's father, Abdulbaset Al-Omary. Physically he was not an unattractive man, yet, from what I knew of his behaviour, I could find nothing to admire.

If only I could reach this man. I would plead for him to return his child to her mother. Unfortunately, Margaret McClain had been unsuccessful in her efforts to discover an address or telephone number for her former husband, and the chances of finding Heidi were slim indeed.

I left New York City in a melancholy frame of mind. Travelling with my family and friends on our private airplane, my mood was sombre. I removed myself from the jovial atmosphere and sat apart from the other passengers.

Sara glanced towards me protectively, but she did not attempt to draw me into the women's circle. Huda was absorbed in a lengthy story of a special dish that she had savoured at Bouley's, one of New York City's finest French restaurants. Sara knew that I found Huda's absurd obsession with food increasingly annoying.

Even in the midst of excited voices, I became lost in my sad thoughts of the innocent children stolen from their mothers.

My thoughts returned to Heidi. What future now awaited this lonely child? From what I had read about Heidi's Saudi father, I knew that the poor girl would be raised in the strictest of Muslim homes. Within a short time she would be compelled to don the veil, for in my country many Muslim girls are being forced to veil even before they reach puberty. Following her veiling, Heidi would undoubtedly be coerced into an arranged marriage to a man she would not know until the first shocking night in the marriage bed.

I tried to sleep, but my rest was fitful. After I had spent a few hours tossing and turning in my uncomfortable seat, Sara came to my side to tell me that we were to land shortly. We would be stopping in London for the night before continuing on to Saudi Arabia.

Had I known that during our short time in England we would be humiliated by the enormous press coverage of a Saudi legal case, I would have pleaded with Kareem to cancel our London landing and instead have the plane fly on to Paris.

Beheaded

Upon arriving at the airport in London, we were confronted with shocking newspaper headlines: the two most prominent words were 'Saudi Arabia' and 'beheadings'.

'What is happening?' I asked Kareem. I was becoming alarmed for my family.

Kareem spoke in a low voice as he guided us through the airport. 'This is the case of those two British nurses. It seems that they have been found guilty of murder.'

'Oh, yes.' I quickly recalled the incident that had attracted so much attention abroad.

The story had begun about a year before when two British nurses, Deborah Parry and Lucille McLauchlan, had been arrested in Saudi Arabia on suspicion of the murder of Yvonne Gilford, an Australian nurse. And now, during the time we had been away in New York City, a Saudi court had found these two women guilty of murder. The British people rejected capital punishment a long time ago, but in Saudi Arabia convicted murderers are still put to death. We were entering a city that was obviously filled with great agitation at the idea of two British citizens losing their heads to the sword of a Saudi Arabian executioner.

I shuddered. Although it is my belief that the crime of murder demands uncompromising punishment, I have always found the idea of beheadings utterly horrifying! Actually, many people find our entire Muslim system of justice primitive and shocking. Islamic law, or *sharia*, is the basis for civil and criminal law in Saudi Arabia: it in turn is based on the Koran and the *sunnah* (examples of Prophet Mohammed's deeds and commands). And, unlike laws in many Western countries, *sharia* stresses the rights of society over the rights of the individual.

The punishments laid down for breaking Islamic laws are swift and severe. Convicted murderers and rapists are beheaded, adulterers are stoned to death, and thieves suffer amputation of their right hand. Other penalties include public lashings, as well as the more universally acceptable jail terms and fines. These severe punishments may look brutal, but most Muslim nations enjoy a lower crime rate than many other countries do.

Knowing that our entire system of justice was under British media scrutiny caused our party to become unusually subdued as our drivers transported us into Greater London.

After we arrived at our apartment in Knightsbridge, Kareem and Asad left for the Saudi Arabian Embassy to find out what was going on. As we settled into our apartment, we women turned our attention to the newspapers Kareem had purchased at the airport.

I winced as I read, for the accounts of the ordeal these two British nurses were undergoing filled the front pages. Every aspect of the Saudi judicial system was explored and condemned. These newspapers seemed to be outraged above all by the idea that our 'primitive' society allows families of murder victims to have a say in the punishment of those condemned.

In Saudi Arabia, if a murder has been committed the family of the victim has the right to demand that the murderer is killed in the same manner, or in any other way they choose. There have indeed been cases of families in Saudi Arabia choosing to inflict the same punishment on the murderer as their loved one had endured, for example, stabbing the condemned to death, or even running him over with a car. However, most Saudis accept the standard sentence of death by beheading.

Families of the victim also have a second option, that of collecting blood money in exchange for sparing the convicted murderer's life. While camels were once used to pay blood money, today the payment is in riyals or dollars. There are set damages according to the circumstances on a scale from 120,000 Saudi riyals to 300,000 Saudi riyals ($45,000 to $80,000). Of course, if the victim is a woman, the blood money is half that for a man.

In this case the two nurses had been found guilty of murdering a third woman. And it was now being reported in British newspapers that the victim's family had been approached about the possibility of accepting blood money for their loved one as provided for under Saudi law, even though the victim's family lived in Australia. The dead woman's brother, Frank Gilford, had reportedly become outraged at the idea that his sister's life could be bought and paid for, and had angrily refused the offer of blood money.

I agreed with Frank Gilford. I, too, would reject the offer of blood money. How can anyone place a monetary value on a life? If only Saudi Arabian men had the same degree of love and esteem for their women as Western men I mused, as I compared Frank Gilford's reaction to a true story that recently had occurred in Saudi Arabia.

This story I was reminded of had unfolded when an inebriated foreigner crashed his automobile into a car carrying female passengers, killing two Saudi women. Two serious crimes had been committed: drinking alcohol and murder, therefore, the foreigner was immediately thrown into jail. He was certain to be condemned to death under Saudi Arabia's strict laws. His only hope was to convince the husband of the dead women to accept blood money. Otherwise, he would be beheaded.

Although other similar cases in Saudi Arabia had shown that most Saudis prefer an 'eye for an eye', the accused's lawyer prepared a plea offering blood money.

When the case was called before the Saudi judge, no-one was more shocked at the reaction of the surviving husband than the guilty foreigner and his lawyer. The husband of the two dead women stood before the judge and said, 'Your honour, I request that the prisoner be released. I do not call for his death, nor do I want his money. The two women killed were wives that I had taken in my youth, and had grown too old to be of service to me.' This man had looked at the defendant and actually smiled. 'I am glad to be rid of them, for now I can replace them with two young wives.'

Under the law, the Saudi judge had no option

but to release the lucky foreigner. It was further reported that the husband actually *thanked* the foreigner, saying that he had wanted to divorce his wives for a long time, but had not wanted to make a financial settlement!

Once again, I considered the good fortune of women of other countries. To be valued and esteemed is beyond the expectations of many Saudi Arabian women.

My attention returned to the fate of the British nurses. Now that they had been convicted, and with execution looming, public interest was at its peak. Although a number of Muslim women have been beheaded in Saudi Arabia, never has a woman from a Western country suffered this cruel fate.

Tension was mounting between the governments of Saudi Arabia and Great Britain. The British were appalled at the possibility that two of their own might be executed, while the Saudis were angered by British criticism of their judicial system.

Huda interrupted my thoughts when she looked up from the newspaper she was reading. 'These English should not complain about our Saudi method of capital punishment. Saeed Al Sayaf, the official executioner, is a skilled swordsman. My husband once witnessed a beheading and spoke of Saeed's work with the highest praise. These British women will be fortunate to have such a practised executioner.' Huda made a clicking sound with her tongue. 'One minute these women will have their heads, and the next minute they will not. They will not suffer *one moment* of pain.'

Sara looked at Huda in horror.

With my hand at my throat, I sat paralysed. I, too, knew something about the swordsman Saeed Al Sayaf, as I had seen him years before being interviewed on Saudi television. I had never forgotten him. Saeed's jovial manner belied his gruesome job. He is an employee of the Ministry of Interior. An executioner since he was a young man, he has wielded his sword many times, and he is now training one of his sons to take his place. For beheadings, Saeed claimed to use a special sword presented to him by Prince Ahmad bin Abdul Aziz Al Sa'ud.

Saeed also carries out punishments for lesser crimes, such as theft. I recalled Saeed explaining that he used sharp knives to cut the wrists of thieves, since it would be difficult to hit the exact spot on a small target such as a wrist with a weapon as large as a sword.

During the interview, Saeed had laughingly claimed that he preferred chopping off heads to cutting off wrists. He also expressed his keen disappointment that the booming economy of Saudi Arabia had lowered the crime rate. There were too few criminals to keep him busy! He had then discussed some of his more memorable beheadings. And, after chopping off more than 600 heads, as well as 60 hands, he had many stories to tell.

The most horrifying story involved two condemned men, partners in crime, who were to be executed together. This was before our current procedure of covering the eyes of the condemned. As a result, the second man watched as Saeed's sword sliced through the neck of his comrade; the severed head fell at his feet. The terrified man looked up and saw that Saeed was preparing his sword to strike him. He fell to the ground in a faint. He was examined by the attending doctor who declared that the man's heart had stopped. As the body of his friend was carried away for burial, the fallen man revived. The swordsman was called back, and the man pleaded to be spared.

I will never forget the wicked smile on the executioner's face as he chuckled at the memory of what must have been one of his better days. Of course, Saeed could not agree to any such thing, and the man was immediately beheaded.

Huda spoke once again. 'These British women are obviously guilty of murder. They should pay for their crime against Allah.'

Sara, with her soft heart, looked at our cousin in disbelief. 'Oh, Huda! Surely you do not mean that.'

'And why not? If a Saudi citizen commits a crime in England, or in America, are they not forced to answer for their crimes?' Huda flicked her fingers in dismissal. 'Do our Muslim laws mean nothing?'

Maysa spoke up as she waved a newspaper in her hand. 'Did you not read this report, Huda? Perhaps these women are innocent. They say here that they were tortured by Saudi policemen. Such things *do* happen, you know.'

Huda flashed her an ugly look. 'Maysa, do not be so naïve. Of course the women did it! They were found guilty in a Saudi court! And what else would a foreign criminal claim, if not police brutality? It is a typical Western trick to escape punishment!'

Huda then rose from her seat and straightened

her dress. 'All this talk makes me hungry. I believe I will have Sultana's cook prepare me this new recipe I found in New York.'

My heretofore hidden distaste for Huda was about to surface. I spoke loudly enough for Huda to hear: 'It appears that the glutton has an insatiable appetite for blood, as well as for food.'

Huda slumped against the wall as if she was stricken with severe chest pains, but we could see she was pretending. Nevertheless, Sara and Maysa ran to her side. As she was being led away, Huda shouted that she was having a heart attack, and that someone should call her husband to tell him to arrange her funeral.

Our maids were alarmed, but I reassured them. 'Do not worry. Although Huda is destined to collapse of a heart attack, her destiny has no connection with my words. Huda's final fate is directly linked to the thick layers of fat that have gathered around her heart.'

The maids began to laugh. Although overweight, Huda was the most robust woman in our extended Al Sa'ud family, and well known for her dramatics. Since she was a young girl, Huda had routinely feigned heart attacks. Most likely, I assured everyone, Huda would enjoy many delicious dishes before she heard God's final summons.

Still smiling, I went into the kitchen to instruct Jada, our London cook and housekeeper, to prepare our dinner.

To my surprise, I found that Jada had already cooked a small feast for us: eggplant salad, lentil soup, pilaw, *kufta* and shish kebab. I saw that this dear girl had even baked Arab bread to please us.

'I'm so happy you are here, ma'am,' she said as she began to load the food onto trays. 'I get lonely, sometimes,' she admitted softly.

I found myself wondering about Jada's life. I had to admit that I knew very little about the girl. While travelling alone to England the year before, Kareem had discovered that our housemaid and one of our drivers were involved in an illicit affair. Since both were wed to others, Kareem terminated their employment and sent them back to their spouses. It was then that he had hired Jada.

I now recalled Kareem telling me that Jada had wept copious tears when pleading for this position, as both maid and cook. She had told him that she came from a poor Egyptian family and must work to help finance an older brother's college education. Although she had arrived with no references, Kareem had sensed a goodness in the girl and had hired her immediately.

I recalled hearing that her parents had emigrated from Egypt years before. After the father was unable to find suitable employment in London, the possibility of a manufacturing job had taken the family to the city of Manchester. Now she lived in London, Jada, who was unmarried, rarely saw her family. Since Kareem and I stay at our home in London no more than once or twice a year, I knew that Jada must spend many long, boring months with few distractions to fill her days.

Looking into Jada's youthful face, I guessed that she was not much older than my youngest daughter, Amani. Yet Jada conducted herself as a mature woman while Amani often displayed child-like conduct. Wealth and privilege too often bring out unattractive attributes, I thought to myself.

And, I must admit, that included me as well.

Through gentle questioning I learned that Jada had been an excellent student at school, and had always longed to become a medical doctor. Her greatest ambition was to return to Egypt and care for pregnant women in the small villages in an effort to lower the high infant mortality of that country, and to combat the practice of female circumcision.

Recently, there had been a great deal of international outrage concerning the custom of female circumcision in Egypt, and Jada was earnest in her desire to help educate women in her land so that they would turn away from that barbaric custom.

'That is an admirable cause,' I told her, as my thoughts went back in time. 'The granddaughter of Fatma, our housekeeper in Egypt, was forced to undergo that brutal practice. Unbelievably, it was the child's *own mother*, Elham, who had insisted upon the inhumane ritual!

'I went with Fatma to try to convince Elham not to subject her daughter to such a dangerous mutilation. But Elham truly believed that our religion demands women to be circumcised, and that her daughter could not defy the laws of her religion.' I sighed heavily, still depressed when I thought of it. 'I agree that educating women is the only solution to end this frightful custom.'

'Women must learn to question authority,' Jada said. 'Otherwise, they will continue to believe everything their fathers and husbands tell them.'

'That is so true,' I agreed.

In view of her own aspirations, I was surprised to learn that Jada felt no animosity about the fact that the whole of her salary was going towards educating her brother. Jada kept only a few pounds a month for herself.

'Once my brother has graduated,' Jada said with a smile, 'then I will ask him to pay for my education.' The dear girl was quietly self-assured that her dreams would come true, and that her brother would honour her wishes as she had so unselfishly honoured his.

I gazed at Jada in fascination. I knew that had I faced the same situation with my brother Ali, I would have made a bonfire with my salary before I would have given it to him. Sadly, I suspected that Jada's dreams might never be fulfilled, for once educated, her brother would most likely wed. Then, the needs of his wife and children would surely take precedence over his sister.

As I walked away, thoughts of Afaaf and Hussah came to my mind. I was struck once more by how the wishes and needs of Arab women are always placed behind the desires of Arab men. There is a terrible truth that permeates Muslim cultures – a truth that few Muslims will ever admit. In *every* Arab or Muslim society, women's lives are like soft wax which men are allowed to twist and stretch according to their individual beliefs and desires.

Since Kareem and Asad did not return from the Saudi Embassy until late in the evening, we women alone enjoyed the feast prepared by Jada. Huda, still angry at my earlier remarks, ate in isolation in her room. As everyone was weary from the rigours of our trip, we retired as soon as we had finished our evening meal.

The following morning, we returned to the airport to continue our journey to Saudi Arabia. We had been out of the kingdom for only eight days, but for some reason the time away seemed endless to me.

Our airplane landed in Jeddah, since Maysa and Huda both live in that city. The rest of us planned to travel on to Riyadh within the next few days. After hearing the tragic story of Heidi, I was anxious to gather Maha and Amani in my arms.

Before retiring that evening in our Jeddah palace, Kareem and I relaxed with a few cocktails. The topic of our conversation was the current crisis between Saudi Arabia and England. Although I attempted to change the subject more than once, Kareem was infused with anger that our country was being criticized for upholding our laws – laws that kept our crime rate substantially lower than most other countries in the world.

All the talk of beheadings distressed me even more than usual, especially because Kareem compared in great detail the barbaric cruelties of the American methods of capital punishment, such as the electric chair and the gas chamber, to the quick and more humane method of beheading.

Moments after we retired, Kareem fell into a deep sleep. I, on the other hand, tossed and turned throughout the night.

For some reason, my mind rested on the tragic fate of a young man by the name of Abdullah Al-Hadhaif, a story which is well-known to every Saudi Arabian. In August 1995 Abdullah Al-Hadhaif was only thirty-three years old, and the father of six young children, when he was executed on the orders of the Saudi government. Along with many other Saudis, Abdullah, his two brothers and his elderly father had been arrested for political crimes, involving personal conduct which offended our government, such as speaking out in the mosques, or distributing leaflets or banned audio tapes.

It was reported that Abdullah's aged father had been tortured while imprisoned, and that his abuse had been so brutal that it had led to a heart attack. Naturally, this had enraged the sons of the elder Al-Hadhaif, and none more than the sensitive Abdullah. When Abdullah was released from prison, he had sought out the secret policeman who had tortured his father. Once that man's identity was known, Abdullah struck back by throwing a container of acid at him. He was injured, but not killed, and was able to identify his attacker.

Once again, Abdullah was thrown into jail. All the festering rage of the Saudi authorities against the protesters focused on this one man. Friends and family of Abdullah reported that he was brutally tortured to obtain a confession. Reports said that he had been dipped in corrosive liquid, to revenge the policeman he had attacked. His bowels were inflated through his anus, and threats were made that his dear mother and precious wife would be sexually violated in his presence.

Still, Abdullah Al-Hadhaif refused to sign the confession.

The fury of his torturers was further heightened by his stubbornness. One report said that Abdullah was hung like a slaughtered sheep with his head tied between his legs. He had been so mercilessly beaten that he was paralysed from his waist down.

I had to admit that the men of my family can be unbelievably heartless! Abdullah's ordeal had ended only when he was beheaded.

What had been that tortured man's final thoughts? I wonder. Had he known fear, and sadness at the thought he would not live to raise his six children? Or, had he been relieved that death would soon bring peace from the agony of his last days? Only God knew the answer to my question.

Many other harrowing images now began to plague my mind. I felt certain that the young child Heidi spent many unhappy hours weeping for her mother. Poor Afaaf was alone in the world. And Hussah legally belonged to a cruel man, as did Munira.

Unable to sleep, I slipped from bed to prepare myself a mixture of rum and cola. Nothing would help but to drink myself into forgetfulness, I decided.

And so I began a long night of heavy drinking. I became so drunk that, during one trip into my closet to conceal an empty bottle, I tripped over my long gown and knocked over a vase. I lunged forward to catch it, but the alcohol had slowed my movements, and the vase smashed against the wall. In the quiet of the night, the noise of the shattering glass vase was deafening.

When Kareem jumped from the bed in alarm, I could not co-ordinate my brain and my tongue to speak out in my defence!

Kareem was instantly aware that his wife was so drunk that she could not speak without slurring her words.

He shouted out in shock. 'Sultana!'

'Oh, Allah!' I mumbled to myself. 'My sins have been discovered!'

I remember nothing else of that moment, for I blacked out, finally obliterating the horrible images that I had tried to drown with drink.

My Secret Revealed

For long hours I stayed in that mysterious realm of darkness when the mind closes down; no information, new or old, is processed. I was not burdened by sorrows, nor was I soothed by pleasing dreams. My brief respite from reality could not last, but I had the pleasure of that dreamless, mindless state until the sounds of the household awoke me the following morning.

When I finally opened my eyes in the harsh light, the first image I saw was Kareem's face. Suddenly, the memory of him waking up and discovering his wife in a drunken state came back to me in a rush. Hoping to redeem last night's disaster with a miracle, I squeezed my eyes tightly shut and prayed to God that what had happened the previous evening had not occurred at all, that it was all a bad dream.

When I looked once more at Kareem, I knew that God had not answered my prayer. Kareem's sad, knowing eyes peeled away any hope that my secret drinking remained hidden from him. Without a word, my husband's expression told me he knew that I was in serious trouble with alcohol.

My husband's clear voice was deceptively calm. 'Sultana, how do you feel?'

I knew full well that my future was now for ever altered, for my destiny was certain to be that of a scorned and divorced wife. I was so filled with horror at this thought that I could not speak.

'Sultana?'

I squeaked, 'I am not so well, husband.'

Kareem nodded.

We stared at each other for a long time without speaking. Neither of us had the heart to attempt further conversation.

In the silence, my presence of mind slowly returned. I quickly reminded myself that I was uncertain as to *exactly* how much Kareem knew of my drinking; that perhaps I should take heed of that wise Arab proverb: 'Your tongue is your horse, and if you let it loose it will betray you.'

I clung to the hope that Kareem believed my drunken state was nothing more than an infrequent occurrence. After all, many were the times throughout our marriage when together Kareem and I had indulged ourselves in drink, and Kareem had never expressed displeasure of this.

'We need to talk, Sultana.'

I remained quiet.

Dropping his gaze, Kareem rubbed his eyes and took a deep breath. 'I have not slept all night.' With a tired sigh, he looked at me once more. 'I have been wondering how you managed to hide this drinking problem from me, and for so long.'

I asked, in that same squeaking tone of voice, 'Drinking problem?'

Ignoring this question, Kareem continued to

stare at me as he softly spoke words that I did not wish to hear.

'Please do not consume our time trying to prove your innocence when you are clearly guilty. I have already spoken with Sara. I now know that you often drink to excess when I am away.'

It was no use to deny it. By the anguished look on his face, I knew Kareem had learned the truth. At the pain of that thought, my chest tightened.

I began to weep. 'Nothing will ever be the same again,' I cried out, wringing my hands. Already, I could imagine the cruel gossip about me that would spread rapidly throughout the extended Al Sa'ud family. My reputation was for ever ruined!

'You cry like a child for what you cannot defend as a woman?'

Kareem's words struck me like a sharp dagger, yet I could not stop weeping. The worst had happened! My desperate need for alcohol had been found out, and I was truly lost. Kareem would divorce me. My children would be humiliated by the scandal. My hated brother, Ali, would be elated that my life had taken a turn for the worse. And my elusive father would feel justified in his dislike of the youngest child born of his first wife even more than he already did. My sobs became even more heartfelt.

My earnest cries softened Kareem's heart. He rose and walked towards me. He sat down on the edge of the bed and began to push my long hair away from my face. 'Darling, I am not angry at you,' he said. 'I am angry at myself.'

I stared in confusion at Kareem. 'Why are you angry at yourself?' I sputtered.

'I failed to see what was in front of me.' He

thoughtfully wiped the tears from my face. 'Had I not been so occupied with business, I would have been aware of your problem long ago. Please forgive me, Sultana.'

Relief swept over me. Kareem was willing to take my burden upon his shoulders. He blamed himself, and not me. I had been saved, once again!

Reckless with the thought of yet another unearned reprieve, I was eager to agree with Kareem, and say that, yes, he had been much too occupied with business matters. He *had* neglected me, his wife. Just as I opened my mouth to express my smugness and feeling of victory, abruptly, I felt the closeness of my mother's spirit in the room. I gasped as I looked around. Although I could not see Mother, I instinctually knew that she was here, witnessing this encounter between my husband and me.

'Sultana, are you all right?' With a look of great concern, he gently stroked my face with his hand.

I nodded, yet still could not utter a sound. The essence of Mother was becoming even stronger. I cannot express the terror I felt when I was struck with the absolute knowledge that I was undergoing some manner of a trial like no other, and that much more was expected of me than my usual immature reactions. A small, silent voice told me that if I were ever again to know genuine peace and joy, I must change my behaviour.

Long moments passed before I could speak. Looking straight at my husband, I said, 'Kareem, I will no longer seek shameful victories. My own weakness, not yours, has created this dilemma. You are blameless. So, erase this worry from your face, husband. I alone am responsible for my drinking.'

There, I had said it! For once in my life, I had not taken the easy means of escape regarding my personal imperfections. Kareem was shocked, as was I, at my new mature accountability.

I smiled at my husband. 'I promise that from this moment, I will make every effort to defeat this problem.'

Kareem took me in his arms. 'Darling, *together* we will defeat this problem.'

Indeed, being in Kareem's loving arms was a great consolation. I did so want to defeat my vexing cravings for alcohol with all its lies and secrecy. Brimming with hope and optimism, my mood quickly became joyful.

Later, Kareem went to find Asad, who was staying at our Jeddah palace with Sara.

Wishing to speak with my sister, I rang through to the guest suite and spoke with Sara on the palace intercom. We agreed to meet in the women's garden.

After embracing my sister, I quickly confided everything that had happened between Kareem and me. Sara was openly happy for me and praised my courage.

She said, 'You should have unburdened your troubles to your husband at the first hint of trouble. I knew that Kareem would not react as you said he might.' She paused before speaking. 'You should have seen him last evening, Sultana. He was completely distraught when he learned that your greatest fear was that he might desert you at your time of need.'

I tried to persuade my sister to tell me everything Kareem had said about me and our marriage, but Sara refused. My husband had spoken to her in confidence.

'We are two fortunate women, Sultana,' she reminded me gently. 'We both married men who are wonderful husbands.' She paused before admitting, 'In this land, such men are as rare as flawless diamonds.'

I thought about Sara's words; what she said was true. Certainly, Asad was a husband unlike any other. He adored my sister. Since the first moment Asad's eyes had seen Sara, no other woman had existed for this former playboy. Sara was the luckiest of women.

And while Kareem had greatly disappointed me on more than one occasion, those painful events had occurred a long time ago. As the years had passed, Kareem had grown into a supportive, loving husband and father. I, too, was a fortunate woman.

After giving my sister a second heartfelt embrace, I returned to my bedroom suite. Kareem walked into the room a few moments later, and with a wide smile, he said that he had an idea that he thought I might like.

I rushed towards my husband and pulled him towards me. He stumbled from the force of my embrace, and we tumbled backwards together onto the bed.

Kareem attempted to speak even as I continued to kiss his lips, his eyes and his nose. 'Sultana, I—'

Just knowing that I had a second chance to redeem my life, I felt like the thief who is told he is going to lose his hand only to discover that the swordsman has died and he has been reprieved. I felt so relieved and joyful that I kissed Kareem until he forgot what idea he wanted to discuss. Soon we were involved in ardent lovemaking.

Later, after Kareem lit a cigarette and passed it back and forth between us, he asked, 'What was that all about?'

I teased, 'Am I not allowed to show my husband how much I love him?'

He smiled. 'Of course, darling. Anytime you are so overwhelmed with this love, call me.'

I laughed, 'Who else would I call?'

Kareem held the cigarette up in the air as he contentedly nuzzled my face with his. 'And, I love you too, darling.'

Kareem placed the cigarette between my lips and waited for me to inhale, before placing it once more between his own lips.

'What was that idea you spoke of?'

'Oh, yes. I have been thinking today that it has been a long time since we took a trip into the desert, together, as a family.' His eyes searched my face for my reaction. 'I believe that you, Sultana, most of all, would benefit from a desert journey into our past.'

What he said was true. While Kareem and Abdullah often joined their royal cousins for jaunts into the desert for hawking and hunting trips, rarely did my daughters and I make such excursions. Thinking back, I realized that it had been several years since our family had retreated to the desert. In the past, such journeys into a simpler way of life, not governed by clocks and calendars, had brought me great mental relaxation.

I could not conceal my feelings. 'Yes,' I said, 'the desert. I would like that, Kareem.'

Although we Saudi Arabs now dwell in ornate palaces and modern cities, we have not forgotten that our recent ancestors were tribal nomads who lived in tents. Actually, today, there are few nomads moving back and forth across the vast Arabian deserts. For the past twenty years or more, the Saudi government has encouraged Bedouin tribesmen to abandon their tents and move into the cities. Yet all Saudi Arabians carry the tribal memory of nomadic travellers in their blood. And although the Al Sa'ud family abandoned the desert long before many of our countrymen, we are no different from other Saudis when it comes to an unrestrained love of the desert.

In 1448 AD, early members of the Al Sa'ud clan withdrew from the harsh desert and began to cultivate the land around the settlement known today as Diriya. The men in our family became successful farmers and traders; in time, they became what are known as city Arabs. Therefore, we Al Sa'uds do not consider ourselves to be nomads, yet we are inexplicably drawn as if to a magnet, to what is, to us, an irresistible sea of endless and sweeping sand.

Kareem interrupted my agreeable musings.

'We will make a family event of this trip,' he said as he watched me. 'We will invite *everyone*.'

Knowing the exact meaning of Kareem's words, I quickly complained, 'Not Ali, I hope!'

Kareem touched my face with his hand. 'Darling, don't you believe that the time has come for you and your brother to put the past behind you? What good does this ceaseless hostility do, for either of you?'

'How can I befriend such a man as Ali? Brother or not, he is too contemptible for words!' I said stubbornly.

'Well, if we invite one, we must invite all.'

I knew that Kareem was right. It would be a shocking insult, a total disregard of Arab hospitality, to invite all our siblings to accompany us to the desert but to deliberately omit Ali and his family. If such an offence were offered, the scandal of our family's estrangement would become the talk of Riyadh.

I sighed deeply. 'Invite him then, if you must. But, I truly dislike the way we Arabs cannot be open about our feelings,' I muttered.

'You were born an Arab princess, Sultana,' Kareem said with a short laugh. 'Why fight your fate?'

What more was there to say?

Despite the hated thought of my brother, I felt more calm than I had in a long time. I lovingly wrapped an arm around Kareem's waist and pulled him close. 'Let's take a short nap,' I suggested.

Although Kareem rarely sleeps in the daylight hours, he too, was weary from our international trip. 'A short rest would be welcome,' he agreed.

As sleep seduced me, I listened to my husband as he softly quoted an old Bedouin creed taught to him by his father. I felt a rush of nostalgia mingled with sadness for a way of life that has disappeared for ever.

> Land that is open wide to wander
> Covered with grass that is fit for grazing
> Ample wells of the sweetest water
> A tent large enough for a large family

A beautiful wife with a sweet temper
Many sons and some daughters
To own great herds of camels
To belong to an honourable tribe
To see Makkah
To live a long life without shame
To be saved from the fires of hell
To enjoy the rewards of paradise!

Lulled by pleasing visions of the simple life once lived by my own ancestors, I drifted off to sleep.

Although my shameful secret had been discovered by my husband, I slept with the serene soundness of a woman who could now look to her future with new hope. Had I known that the following day would bring forth yet another family drama, creating one of the most alarming moments of my life, I am certain that my afternoon nap would have been much less restful.

Threat to the Throne

While Kareem was enjoying his morning shower, I lingered under the bed covers, moving restlessly from side to side. I missed our daughters terribly and was anxious to leave Jeddah and return to Riyadh.

As the rushing sound of the water flow from Kareem's shower ceased, I arose from bed and walked towards the balcony adjoining our bedroom suite. Pushing aside the window shade, I looked outside. The view was just as I expected. It was a typical day in Saudi Arabia, bright and sunny.

Within a few moments, Kareem was out of the shower and standing beside me. He made an attempt to caress my breasts with his hands.

Several years before, I had travelled to Switzerland for a breast reconstruction to replace the breast I had lost to cancer during the early years of our marriage. As part of the medical rehabilitation, I had been told that the breast must be massaged daily in order to keep the liquid ingredients that formed my new breast soft and supple. Since that time, Kareem had insisted that he should be the one to take responsibility for my therapy.

An inviting smile spread across his face. 'Do you want to go back to bed, Sultana?'

I returned his smile but said, 'No, darling. Truthfully, I want nothing more than to see the beautiful faces of our two daughters.'

My husband's smile faded, but he understood. 'Yes, of course. I miss them, also.' He paused. 'Telephone Nura and tell her that we will arrive in Riyadh later this afternoon. Have her drivers deliver the children home from school.'

Soon we were at the airport and ready to board our plane for the short flight from Jeddah to Riyadh. Once we had arrived, Sara and I said hasty farewells as we got into separate automobiles. Sara was as anxious as I to see her own children.

Maha and Amani were waiting for us. After heartfelt hugs and greetings, I gave our daughters the gifts that I had purchased for them in New York. Both daughters received many new clothes, some electronic gadgets, music CDs, movie videotapes and books.

Kareem then said that he had work to do. I was further disappointed when both Amani and Maha expressed a desire to return to their own suites and return telephone calls from their friends. I had some difficulty convincing them to stay a while longer with their mother.

Once my children became teenagers they began to prefer the company of their peers to their own mother, and I had often wished that I possessed a great power that could move back time so that I could once again enjoy the days when my children were babies.

Smiling, I held out my arms in invitation and

said, 'Let us sit together for a while. Then you can go and make your calls.'

I called out for one of our servants to serve us with some cold *laban*, their favourite, buttermilk-like drink.

Maha smiled, then snuggled against me on the large sofa that faced the television set. Amani curled up into an oversized chair.

Maha yawned and picked up the TV remote control to switch on the television set. Several years before, Kareem had purchased a large satellite dish to capture television channels from all over the world. It is illegal in Saudi Arabia to possess a satellite dish. Our government insists upon censoring the information its citizens see, hear, or even read. However, this decree is ignored by people wealthy enough to purchase and import satellite dishes, partly because the limited programming fare offered by Saudi television is so boring! Certainly we were not interested in the sanitized news reports and endless self-congratulatory accounts of the good deeds performed by members of our own royal family that were all that were available on Saudi channels.

The religious authorities in Saudi Arabia are also against satellite dishes, for a different reason. Religious men fear that good Muslims will be adversely influenced by images from the decadent West. It is not unusual for a committee of *mutawwas*, or religious men, to roam the streets of Saudi cities looking for satellite dishes. Although homes in Riyadh are surrounded by walls, their flat rooftops are usually visible from the street.

The *mutawwas* go from street to street, examining rooftops. Should a television satellite dish be discovered, these men attempt to destroy the dish by any means possible. Rocks and sticks are thrown at the satellite dish, and if that fails, rocks and sticks are thrown at the *owners* of the dishes. Just a year ago, a group of unruly *mutawwas* became so incensed by the presence of a television satellite dish that they fired bullets at it! A poor Indian woman was on the roof hanging laundry. When the *mutawwas* began to discharge their firearms, the woman was shot in the abdomen. Thankfully, she survived her injury.

Since that incident, Saudi owners of satellite dishes have gone to great lengths to hide their equipment. Today, many flat rooftops in Arabia are completely surrounded by sheets, hanging from high steel poles, to block the view of the rooftop from the street. But this camouflage has merely encouraged the *mutawwas* to fire at the sheets themselves.

Of course, as Al Sa'uds, we do not have to concern ourselves with the unpleasant activities undertaken by the *mutawwas*.

When Maha paused to watch an English comedy show depicting a woman ridiculing a man, I noticed Amani's lip curling in repulsion. In the Arab world, no woman would ever poke fun at her husband in view of another, or depict a woman as more intelligent than a man.

Without warning, Amani leaped to her feet and grabbed the remote control.

'Mother!' Maha screamed her objection.

This was not the afternoon of pleasure and relaxation with my daughters that I had anticipated. I gestured with my hand for Amani to pass the control to me.

In an effort to appease both daughters, I began switching from channel to channel, searching for a suitable programme that would entertain everyone. Quite unexpectedly, I came upon a news story on a British channel about Professor Mohammed Al Massari, a Saudi citizen who had greatly outraged all in the Al Sa'ud family. Instantly, I became so focused on the broadcast that Amani and Maha were forgotten.

The professor was a Saudi scholar whose subversive ideas for the democratization of Saudi Arabia had severed him from his own country. After being arrested and imprisoned, he was released but was continuously harassed by the Saudi authorities. He had escaped Saudi Arabia the previous year and sought refuge in England. Since that time, he had organized a band of Saudi Arabian exiles into a London-based organization that called itself 'The Committee for the Defence of Legitimate Rights'. To appease their fury at the injustices they had suffered, this group of dissidents had recently drawn Western media attention by describing the alleged corruption of our Saudi royal family. Indeed, these disclosures undoubtedly caused many sleepless nights in Al Sa'ud palaces. This man had exposed so many family secrets that my relatives were left wondering how he could possibly have obtained such confidential information. Had some people working for our family become spies for our enemies?

Mohammed Al Massari's allegations included that certain high-ranking members of the ruling family routinely embezzled millions of riyals, from paybacks on foreign contracts to the confiscation of valuable land belonging to ordinary citizens. He claimed that these cheated people were too frightened to protest, for they feared arrest and imprisonment on false charges. It was alleged that all this corruption has created more than fifty billionaires in my own extended family.

I found everything Al Massari claimed hard to believe, although I could not deny corruption was rife in some branches of our family. For example, a prominent princess, a cousin whom I know quite well, often laughingly boasts about the scandalously inflated rent she collects by renting buildings to the Saudi military.

What makes me so indignant is that there is no need for such behaviour. The monthly allowance received by all royals far exceeds our needs. With each prince and princess receiving 35,000 Saudi riyals ($10,000) monthly, a large branch of the family can collect several hundred thousand dollars each month.

There were other allegations. This professor and his associates also accused certain foreign journalists from highly regarded newspapers and magazines of being paid handsome bribes to vilify and slander other writers who dare write the truth about our government and our country. And here was Mohammed Al Massari, speaking out freely on British television, broadcast all over the world, while a reporter listened with interest and sympathy!

I sprang to my feet and stood before the television set.

When Maha started to speak, I hushed her. 'Shhh, look,' I said as I leaned forward. I wanted to commit this traitor's face to memory. The physical appearance of this enemy of my family would surely match the evil portrait that already formed in my mind. But I saw a dignified man whose eyes flashed with intelligence. Judging by his genial appearance, an observer would never dream that there was anything particularly important on the man's mind, certainly not such desperate ideas as over-throwing a king. Here was a disturbing man!

Kareem had spoken more than once about this professor. He was considered an ominous threat to the rule of the Al Sa'uds, and the throne that allowed my family to claim the country, and its revenues, as their own. I knew that my husband, father, brother, cousins and uncles would go to extreme measures to protect their right to control the oil of Arabia – the black gold that currently flowed in a thousand streamlets directly into the coffers of the royal clan.

My mind raced as I listened. The interviewer appeared to approve of the fact that England was becoming a haven for Middle Eastern dissidents such as Professor Al Massari. But I felt that British citizens might one day regret offering sanctuary to opponents of oil-rich governments, for the men of my family are extremely vengeful. After all, a Saudi government vendetta against the people of Britain had already occurred. In 1980, Princess Misha'il, the granddaughter of Prince Mohammed, was put to death in Saudi Arabia for the crime of adultery. A film dramatization of her story, *Death of a Princess*, made by an independent television company had been broadcast in Britain.

When King Khalid learned the contents of the film, he was embarrassed and outraged by the film's depiction of Saudi royalty. He temporarily severed diplomatic ties with Great Britain, recalling the Saudi ambassador to London and sending the British ambassador to Saudi Arabia packing. More seriously, contracts with British firms worth millions of pounds were cancelled with the consequence that many British jobs were lost.

When the broadcast ended, I returned to my chair and slowly sipped my drink of cold *laban*. Mohammed Al Massari looked nothing like I had imagined, I mused. Instead, he looked the scholar he was, not the rebel he had become.

Maha took the remote control from my hand and switched to a channel that was showing music videos. Amani's face was set like granite as she stared into nothingness.

I gripped one hand in the other and murmured out loud, 'What caused that man to hate us so? Why risk his reputation, his liberty and the well-being of his family, all for an *idea*?'

Maha murmured, 'I don't know, Mother.'

Amani came to life with a self-satisfied smile as she said, '*I* know.'

I sat astonished, and looked dumbly at Maha, who also looked puzzled. Amani's words triggered a stream of speculations in my mind. 'What do you know of *that* man, Amani?'

'Do you *really* want to know?'

Desperate thoughts of Amani allied to some forbidden political organization sank into my mind like a dagger. I stared at her before finally shouting, 'Your mother *demands* to know!'

'All right,' she said, as if proud of her special knowledge.

Unspoken ideas were running through my mind. My daughter is part of a rebellion! Whatever will Kareem and I do?

Amani cleared her throat before she began speaking. 'You asked why the professor was willing to risk everything? The reason is simple, Mother. The professor grew up in a family which has always questioned our family's claim to the throne.'

Drenched with anxiety for my daughter, I wiped my forehead and upper lip with a tissue. I could hold my tongue no longer. 'Wait, Amani.' I spoke in a dry croak. 'Are *you* a member of this banned organization?'

Stillness hung in the room, no-one spoke.

'Amani!' I shouted.

My daughter pulled herself up in the seat and tucked her legs beneath her. She stared boldly into my eyes, luxuriating in the agony she was inflicting upon her visibly shaken mother.

A great sadness gripped my heart. I cannot deny that Amani is a lovely girl. She is doll-like and petite with a perfectly shaped figure. Her skin is the colour of honey and she has a dainty straight nose, full pink lips, perfect white teeth and velvety chocolate eyes widely spaced under arched, slanting brows. Yet, even though my daughter grows more beautiful with each passing year, her personality has become more and more uninviting. As the years have passed, I have become convinced that internal beauty is more important for living a happy life than external beauty, therefore, I knew that I would dearly like to turn Amani inside out.

Finally, just as I was about to grab my child and

shake her, she gave me a squinting smirk and waved her hand in the air.

'No, Mother. Don't worry.' She narrowed her eyes as she spoke, 'Women play no role in the professor's movement. I am not wanted.'

'*Alhamdulilah!*' 'Praise God!' For the first time in my life, I was glad to hear that females were excluded.

Amani raised her voice. 'I learned all I know from a friend whose brother distributes documents and tapes for this organization. The brother is a zealous supporter of the professor and knows everything about his life. He told her what I am telling you.'

Regaining my composure, I looked at Maha and said, 'We women must remember that our own family can do more for females in Saudi Arabia than any other individual can. Surely this man's talk of fighting for democratic rights will evaporate in the heat of the desert; in any case, where women's rights are concerned, he is obviously a typical Saudi man.'

I turned my attention back to Amani. 'The professor's organization has no use for women. You said so yourself.'

In a slow, provoking tone, Amani asked, 'You said you wanted to know about this man. Do you still?'

'I want to know everything *you* know about this man, Amani.'

'Well.' Amani bit her lip in concentration. 'Where was I?'

Maha spoke, 'The rebel's family has always questioned our family's right to the throne.'

'Oh, yes. Coming from a family who fostered

democracy, the professor was determined to help create reform. He waited on the government to introduce reform, but he waited in vain.'

Although I was beginning to have some respect for this Al Massari, even agreeing that *some change* is in order, I have never wished for my family to lose their power. And, while Mohammed Al Massari might be a man of brilliant thoughts, I suspected that he might find it difficult to hold a country together that had been created decades ago by a warrior genius.

The country of Saudi Arabia is made up of many different factions, including the uneducated Bedouin class, wealthy business families and middle-class professionals. It is difficult enough for our family, which has been in power since Saudi Arabia's creation, to keep such a diverse group of citizens happy, without having to concede democratic reforms.

I turned my attention back to my daughter's droning voice.

'The professor was unable to convert others to his way of thinking. But, when Iraq invaded Kuwait, everything changed. We Saudis were stunned to discover that we could not defend ourselves, and that we needed foreign armies to come into our country to save us. Suddenly, with the presence of foreign armies, ordinary Saudis finally became politicized. Many Saudi Arabians were heard to say that the presence of foreign armies in their beloved land was so shameful that it was the final nail in the coffin of the House of Al Sa'ud.'

With her hands, Amani pretended to hammer that nail.

'And so, Uncle Fahd lost his own people when he embraced the Western enemy.'

'That's simply not true, Amani,' Maha exclaimed in protest. '*All* Saudis love the King!'

Amani gave her sister a condescending smile, but did not bother to argue Maha's claim.

Remembering the very real fear that Saddam Hussein, our Arab neighbour and former friend, might actually bomb our cities, I quoted an Arab proverb, 'Never forget, Amani, a prudent enemy is safer than a reckless friend!'

An increasingly curious Maha now asked her sister, 'And so, what else do you know, Amani?'

Amani shrugged her small shoulders. 'The rest of the story is known by everyone. The moment Western armies arrived on our soil, Saudis began to rise from a long sleep. Intellectuals began to participate in clandestine meetings, and an opposition group was formed.'

I sniffed. What Amani said was true. Every Saudi Arabian knew that a committee of dissidents, composed of fifty men, including scholars, businessmen, judges and religious leaders had written a letter to the King. This letter called for an end to oppression, and asked for participation in the running of the government. Over four hundred prominent Saudi Arabians added their signatures to the dissidents' document. When this letter was presented to the King, it is said he went into shock before consulting the Council of the Senior Scholars. On orders from the King, this council had condemned the committee, saying it should be abolished and the members punished. The secret police arrested the professor and jailed him at Al Hayir Prison, located a few kilometres outside of Riyadh.

Amani spoke once again. 'I do know that for six months Professor Al Massari was kept imprisoned, partly in solitary confinement.'

Maha clicked her tongue in sympathy.

I gave her a sharp look. 'Do not forget, daughter, this man is calling for the downfall of your own family.'

Maha's face reddened as she looked away.

'I was told by my friend that this professor was tortured while in prison,' Amani continued. 'While under interrogation, prison guards spat in his face, beat his feet with a bamboo cane, pulled his beard and boxed his ears.'

I stared at my hands, listening, ashamed, knowing that such events are routine in Saudi prisons.

'My friend also told me that the professor was charged with heresy. Of course, when told to confess, he refused.

'The High Court could not agree upon an action. They were obviously dealing with a man of courage, and the law said they must either behead him, or release him. Since they were fearful of creating a martyr, the professor was given a chance to appeal his case. He was told that he would be released and given a chance to reflect upon his actions. If he kept away from political controversy, he might remain free.'

Such is the way of my family, I thought. They always hope that problems will simply vanish. If only all the dilemmas of life were so simple!

'Well, of course, the professor is not a man who can be silenced, so immediately on his release he began to participate in the committee's actions again. A secret source warned the professor that the capital charge of treason was being prepared against him. The committee agreed that the time had come for the professor to leave Saudi Arabia, and continue his fight from abroad. An elaborate escape plan was prepared.'

I felt a flutter in my heart. Was my own daughter privy to secret information about his escape?

'The professor and a friend came up with a ruse to visit an ill friend confined in hospital. Inside the hospital, they were met by a third man who bore a striking physical resemblance to the professor and who changed places with him. When the two men left, the government agents trailing the professor followed the wrong man. No longer followed, it was easy for the professor to get to Riyadh airport. With a false passport, he flew to a small town on the Yemeni border. He waited for two days for his Yemeni contacts, men who knew a route which avoided border controls. The small secret group crossed the Saudi–Yemeni border on foot. In Yemen, there were new contacts waiting to assist him on his journey to London.'

Amani's voice came across low and heavy. 'Of course, everyone knows that when the professor escaped, his own son and brothers were taken as hostages by our family and imprisoned.' Amani flopped back into the easy chair, expelling a deep breath. 'And, that's the story of the professor. Practically everyone under the age of thirty in our country knows this, and now, many, many young people secretly support Professor Al Massari.'

I moved my head slowly and heavily. Was this why sit-ins and demonstrations were disrupting the peace of the land? Soon, I feared, the entire country would share the professor's urgent demands for change.

'We Al Sa'uds are doomed,' I moaned, as I buried my head in my hands.

Kareem's Prophecy

At that very moment, Kareem entered the room.

Concerned, he asked our daughters, 'What is wrong with your mother?'

Maha blurted out, 'Mother is worried that Amani is a member of a revolutionary group.'

Confusion surged in Kareem's eyes, and, for a short period of time, words flew this way and that without anyone really understanding what was happening. Once he realized that Amani had more information than she should have had of the man who was calling for our family's downfall, Kareem became a man wildly possessed.

First, he screamed at Amani, telling her that, 'Daughter! Have you lost all good sense? Are you a follower of this man?'

Amani protested her innocence. 'I am not a follower! I simply reported what I have been told.' My daughter stared coldly into my face. 'Mother insisted that I tell. It's her fault!'

'Forget what your mother said! You must not be associated with *anyone* who has taken up the cause of our most vocal enemy! Arrests are happening every day!' Kareem pounded the wall with his fists, causing the expensive paintings to vibrate. 'You stupid, stupid, stupid child!'

Alarmed, I watched as Amani chewed the inside of her mouth.

I was about to comfort my child when Kareem directed the greater force of his anger towards me! 'Sultana! You have raised your daughters to be rebels! I tell you, I won't put up with it a moment longer!'

I was so shocked at Kareem's accusation that I could not speak.

Maha slipped from the room, and Amani tried to leave with her, but Kareem ordered her to stay.

'Wait here, Father, I have something that will interest you.' Amani spun on her heels and quickly left the room.

Kareem stood frozen like a stone.

In my uneasiness, I circled the room.

Amani returned with a briefcase, which she silently handed to her father.

Kareem's anger was obviously growing by the minute, for he fumbled with the briefcase lock. Once he had opened it, he examined one paper after another, discarding sheet after sheet on the floor. I had never seen Kareem in such a state of agitation.

'Where did you get these papers?' he bellowed at Amani.

'My friend stole them from her brother's room,' she confessed.

'Here!' Kareem shoved a stack of papers into my reluctant hands.

I picked up a packet of cigarettes and toyed with the pack as I tried to focus on the printed pages. After lighting a cigarette, I finally calmed myself to the point that I could understand the significance of the papers I held in my hand.

I quickly saw that the papers were copies of actual press releases and documents written by Dr Al Massari and other Saudi dissidents. The document I selected to read was entitled 'Prince of the Month' which was an exposé of the alleged activities of one of my older cousins, who was a province governor. The document claimed that, 'He has been overheard to say in the *majlis* (the open house where citizens bring complaints to their governor) "The tribes of the south have the mentality of slaves, I fill their bellies and mount their backs." And, "My grandfather Adbul-Aziz told me that the people of this province are a combination of apes and slaves." '

The writer of this document went on to accuse my cousin of various sins, including the appropriation of huge tracts of province land which he then sold for a huge profit.

As I rushed through the documents, I saw that each page contained at least one savage indictment of an uncle or a cousin. One cousin was even implicated in a *murder*! An accountant for Saudi Airlines had been beaten to death after he had presented a bill for millions of riyals to this cousin. Of course, nobody had ever been charged with this crime.

Any detachment that I hoped to maintain rapidly vanished when I saw the name of my own father. I held my hand against my mouth to keep from crying out as I quickly read over a litany of vile deeds attributed to him. My heart sank, for I suspected that some of the denunciations could easily be true. Overcome with sad thoughts of my father, I looked at the faces of my husband and child. A hundred questions rose in my mind, but one look at Kareem's drawn face and my questions died on my lips.

However, Amani bravely burst out, 'Father, is this true?' She gripped tightly to the document she was showing Kareem. 'Does our Al Sa'ud family arrest *children*?'

Her query brought me to my feet. Looking over Amani's shoulder, I softly read, 'Last week Fahd Al-Mushaiti, age eleven years, and Mansour Al-Buraydi, age twelve years, were detained in Buraydi and charged with carrying leaflets that had angered Al Sa'ud. It would seem that the Al Sa'uds have conveniently forgotten that they are repeating the crimes of Saddam Hussein, against whom they have previously fought. They have also forgotten that their newspapers, even today, still criticize his actions.'

Our defiant daughter persisted. 'Father, answer me, does our family really arrest children?'

Kareem withdrew the document from Amani's hand. He did not answer.

A tearful Amani persisted. 'Father?'

Kareem began stuffing the papers back into the briefcase. In a flat voice he retorted, 'You know that our enemies lie.'

'Much of what I read was true, husband.'

Seething like a pot on a hot fire, Kareem flashed an angry look in my direction.

'But greatly exaggerated, of course,' I added quickly.

Kareem then tried to recover every document, but I hid the ones in my hands behind my back. 'I want to read one particular section again,' I said. 'I'll return them to you later in the evening.'

After inhaling several deep, ragged breaths, Kareem turned his attention back to Amani. 'I won't ask you to name who provided you with these documents, but only on the condition that you banish these people from your life.'

Amani's voice was shrill. 'But, father, she's my friend!'

'This is an order, child! I will not have my own daughter fraternizing with our enemies!'

Amani began to weep, but Kareem did not soften his stance. 'Amani?'

After some moments, she gave her word. 'I promise, Father.'

Frightened into submission Amani whispered in her father's ear before receiving a heartfelt embrace, and then left the room.

Kareem's penetrating eyes were now turned on me. He mimicked the sound of my voice, 'Much of what I read was true, husband!' He glowered, 'A wife who upholds her husband is a great treasure, Sultana!'

Only recently had I learned that a cunning warrior knows when to retreat. Unable to rival Kareem's intense fury, and fearful of provoking him even further, I hurried from the room.

Kareem stormed out of the palace. When he did not return for our evening meal, I knew that I would not see him again until late.

I looked in on the children and found that an unusually subdued Amani had retired early. Maha was talking on the telephone.

I stared at the clock and waited for my husband. As I waited, I read once more the vituperative accusations against many prominent members of my family. I read of allegations of adulterous behaviour, theft, acts of repression, false arrests and arrogant disregard for the responsibilities of the elevated station that we Al Sa'uds had been fortunate to inherit.

My suspicion that there was truth in these allegations depressed me. This low state of mind soon led me to imagine that Kareem was at that moment in the arms of another woman. Many Al Sa'ud princes are guilty of bringing women of questionable moral character into our country for the illicit sexual pleasure they offer. Haunted by visions of my beloved caressing another, I began to wander restlessly around the room. In an outburst of frustration, I smashed a crystal vase against the wall. Even this provided no relief, and I began to cry.

Sleep escaped me. Just as I finally closed my eyes, the light shining through the cracks between the window shades revealed that it was dawn.

Kareem did not return home until mid-morning.

I was preparing to telephone Kareem's brother, Asad, when my husband walked through the door. Despite his red-rimmed eyes, Kareem had the expression of a man who was merely returning from a routine errand.

'Sweetheart,' he said, as he bent to kiss me.

My calm smile concealed my despair. Every woman has a hidden source of knowledge about her husband. I smelled the scent of another woman on my husband, and told him so.

In an attempt to placate me, Kareem spun one lie after another, but in a jealous fury, I dragged three suitcases into our bedroom.

I packed my clothes.

Kareem unpacked my clothes.

I packed, and he unpacked.

Our conversation went the same way as our packing, with everything repeated in different words.

I stared into my empty bag, and threatened divorce.

Kareem held the phone and told me to dial a certain number, that he had been at the home of a friend, and that the friend would swear to the truth that they had been without female companionship.

Knowing that such a friend would protect him, I understood that I would never know the truth. 'Why should I cook water?' I asked scornfully. 'It will only remain water.'

Temporarily defeated by the freedom only men can claim as their own, I felt a desperate urge to inflict pain on my husband. Remembering the vow I had made to defeat my drinking habit, and knowing that Kareem would be greatly wounded were I to break it, I walked to the cabinet that held our store of liquor. Uncapping a bottle of whisky, I drank straight from the bottle. My eyes met Kareem's shocked stare. I told him what was on my mind: 'Husbands rule, wives endure.' I paused as I took another swallow, then threatened, 'If you go to bed with other women, Kareem, then I will certainly become an alcoholic.'

Kareem blinked in surprise, then said, 'Ah! A drink,' as he glanced at his watch. 'At ten o'clock in the morning! What a wonderful idea, Sultana.' He walked towards me, took the bottle from my hand, and then he, too, took a long drink from the bottle.

With the back of his hand he wiped his lips and moustache. 'If the woman I love becomes an alcoholic, then I will become one too!'

I stared at Kareem. I had no desire for either of us to become alcoholics!

The faintest of smiles began to flicker across Kareem's face. My husband is a man of two distinct parts, one lovable and one detestable. I began to weaken after looking into his large black eyes filled with so much affection.

When Kareem's massive chest began to rise and fall with silent laughter, my anger evaporated. I laughed aloud as I put the bottle of alcohol back into the cabinet.

Suddenly, we were locked in a lovers' embrace. Our latest disagreement was quickly buried in the same bottomless container as every other unresolved issue of our marriage.

The following morning a serious Kareem said that he had to speak with me about an important matter. After ordering a strong coffee from the kitchen, I sat quietly, sipping from my cup, listening as Kareem shared his thoughts.

'The incident with Amani has caused me to rethink my ideas on Saudi Arabia's future. I have decided to invest more of our money into foreign ventures.'

I stared blankly before responding. 'Why would you do that?'

'For the sake of our children, Sultana.' He paused. 'Do you agree?'

Trying to think, I rubbed my forehead with my fingers.

'Well, I don't know. It's too early to think about business.' I paused before adding, 'Don't you think we already own enough businesses abroad?'

Kareem and I owned hotels and businesses in Europe, America and Asia. Even now, to keep watch over all that we owned was nearly impossible. Following a recent accounting, we were told that our total assets in real estate, cash and businesses worldwide, were nearly 900 million dollars.

Kareem leaned in towards me. 'Listen to me, Sultana. It's time to face reality. Even our *own* daughter, the *niece* of the King, is critical of the regime. Can you imagine what other Saudis think of our family? Sultana, one day, we are going to lose Saudi Arabia. Perhaps not in our lifetime, but certainly during the lifetimes of our children.'

My husband's words depressed me, although this was a topic our family had discussed on many occasions before.

'Nothing lasts for ever,' Kareem mused. 'Our family will eventually lose its control. I greatly fear that Saudi Arabia will tread the same path taken by Iran and Afghanistan. The Islamic fundamentalist ripple is growing into a tidal wave that will engulf every Muslim country.' Kareem paused while gathering his thoughts.

The idea of Saudi Arabia going the way of Afghanistan caused my heart to pound with fear. The sad story of Afaaf, Sara's maid, made one thing quite clear. Should Saudi Arabia ever be ruled by fundamentalists, Saudi women's lives would become even *more* oppressed.

Kareem's voice became bitter. 'Besides, the only reason we're still in power today is because the

United States needs Saudi oil. One day that need will be filled by some other fuel source. Already scientists are starting to find substitutes for the fuel needs of the West. When that day comes, Saudi Arabia – and our family – will be expendable to the Americans.'

Kareem's face became blotched with anger. 'All American politicians are self-serving. They'll throw us to the jackals the moment our usefulness is gone, in the same manner they discarded Mohammed Reza Shah Pahlavi.' Kareem looked at me sadly. 'Sultana, my estimate is that within twenty years, we all will be living in exile.'

I stared at Kareem. 'Even if we no longer rule,' I whispered, 'could we not live in quiet obscurity in our own country?'

'No,' Kareem sighed. 'We will be burdened with our name. A fundamentalist regime will rule. Saudi Arabia will be too dangerous for any Al Sa'ud. We will be hated by everyone.'

I knew that what my husband was saying was true. We have a saying that 'Arabs are either at your feet or at your throat,' and I knew that in one swift moment our fortunes could be reversed. We Al Sa'uds will rule, or we will be destroyed; there will be no in-between.

Kareem shook his head wearily. 'We've got no-one to blame but ourselves, Sultana. What have we done to endear ourselves to the religious leaders? Nothing! What have we done to reassure the business community? Nothing! Our fathers do not listen to their sons. A few concessions here and there would do no harm. It would make our position stronger. But, no. Our fathers are deaf. They can hear nothing but the ghost of their own father, a man who thought of himself as the hammer, and his subjects as the nails.'

I nodded in agreement. Everyone knew that Grandfather Abdul Aziz, the Bedouin warrior who had created the Kingdom of Saudi Arabia in 1932, had ruled his family and the citizens of his country with a firm hand.

Kareem slapped his hands together before leaning back in his chair. 'It's hopeless, Sultana.'

Tears of sadness began to roll down my face.

Kareem searched his pockets for a handkerchief. 'Sultana, please do not cry.'

I buried my nose in Kareem's handkerchief. I knew that everything he had said was true, and that one day I would lose the only life I had ever known. This, because the elders of our family were too stubborn and too foolish to understand change is often necessary just to maintain the situation one has. And why couldn't the Al Sa'uds better control the current climate of nepotism, corruption and wasteful outlay that so enraged the citizens of Saudi Arabia? Every person in the Al Sa'ud clan was already rich and powerful beyond imagination. Even if they never made another Saudi riyal, the members of my family could still live a hundred lifetimes in unbelievable splendour.

My tears continued to flow.

Kareem whispered, 'Sultana, darling, please stop crying.'

Much to Kareem's relief, I finally managed to control my tears, but nothing could relieve my fear of what our future would hold.

Wadi al Jafi

Three weeks later our palace in Riyadh was bustling with excited servants as they rushed past each other. They were finishing the chores necessary to launch our family's excursion into the desert. Many of them were to accompany us to the desert, a rare diversion from their routine lives. Combined with the boisterous activities of the servants were the shouts of rambunctious workmen who sweated profusely as they loaded furniture and heavy equipment onto large moving vans.

Although everyone was delighted at the prospect of spending time in the desert, members of my family are never willing to forgo our opulent lifestyle. Accustomed to luxurious living, we have no desire to emulate the harsh living conditions endured by our desert ancestors.

Now, along with black Bedouin tents and custom-made furniture, workmen were loading Persian carpets, silk cushions, luxurious linens, fine china, crystal glassware, silver cutlery, as well as the more mundane pots and pans. Bathroom equipment specially designed for travelling, including bathtubs, toilets and basins, waited to be packed. Once these items were loaded, the designer trunks containing our wardrobes would be packed last for easy access.

Five gas-powered generators had already been loaded into a separate truck. They would power the two solidly packed large freezers, and the three refrigerators, waiting to be loaded. Two gas stoves and gas cylinders stood beside them.

Our Filipino gardeners were in charge of packing fresh food, including fruits and vegetables imported from Egypt, Jordan and Italy. Over 1,000 bottles of Evian mineral water waited to be lifted into a separate truck. Two large tanker trucks stood ready for our departure, filled with water for cooking and bathing.

In the background, I could hear the bleats and squawks of sheep and chickens, recently delivered from the animal bazaar. After an hour of standing in the hot sun on the truck bed, these poor creatures were becoming impatient and noisy. There were camels, too, some for riding, while some unlucky others would be prepared as a desert feast.

I made a mental note to keep the sensitive Amani as far away as possible from the area where these beasts would be slaughtered. She would be devastated if she witnessed the killing of any animal.

The previous week, Kareem had arranged for twenty-five new air-conditioned four-wheel-drive vehicles to be delivered to our palace to transport our large party.

Loud and angry words rang out across the garden. One of our three Egyptian cooks was shouting obscenities at one of the kitchen apprentices.

Hawkers, the men who train and tend to Kareem's prized falcons, were walking around the garden with their hooded charges perched on their upraised hands, protected by leather gloves, called *dasma al tair*, because the falcons' hooked claws are capable of ripping flesh to the bone. With their powerful eyes, long and pointed wings, strong hooked bills and long curved talons, falcons will easily bring down desert rabbits, wild pigeons and the *hubara*, a large migratory bird also known as a bustard. The falcons were outfitted with a leather *burqa*, or hood. Specially made hawk stands, called *wakar al tair*, were placed around the garden. The Arabian Peninsula is one of the last places on earth where men hunt with falcons. The winter season was not yet quite over, so our husbands planned to hunt while in the desert.

In the midst of all this activity, Maha and I looked at each other in mutual understanding before we burst out laughing. The combination of all these colourful sights and clamorous noises made our garden appear as exotic as a bustling bazaar.

Even Amani began to smile, although she was caught up in giving special instructions to a dispirited Filipino maid regarding the feeding and grooming of her numerous pets during her absence. This maid had just learned that she was one of the ten unlucky employees designated by Kareem to remain behind at our palace in Riyadh.

Although I never tire of watching such sights, I had yet to take my morning bath, so I walked back inside the palace. Considering the uncomfortable heat of the sun outside, I told one of the housemaids to pack an extra supply of sun cream.

After taking a bath and softening my skin with a thick lotion, I dressed in an ankle-length, light blue cotton dress. We Saudis dress in the desert as we do in the city, the men covered up from the intense sun by *thobes* and the women by long dresses.

I then braided my long hair before laying out my veil, headscarf and *abaaya*. When we left our private grounds, I would be obliged to cover myself in these items of clothing.

I fingered the silky garments with a sense of dislike and dread. On trips abroad, I always gratefully discard the despised black coverings, but in Saudi Arabia, they are a hated part of my everyday life. After looking at the world minus a black screen, and breathing fresh air without a fabric filter, the veil always feels like the weight of the world falling around my body, although it is made of thin, gauzy cloth. I sighed deeply. I was a grown woman, but I was still confused by the contradictions in my life. I pushed aside these unpleasant thoughts before returning to the garden.

Those siblings and their families who would accompany us on this trip had already arrived, and when our drivers started up the engines, our large party began to crowd around the vehicles.

My sisters, Sara, Nura, Tahani, Dunia and Haifa, rode with me in one vehicle, while our husbands rode in two others. Our children banded together into groups and commandeered their own jeeps. After all the family members were seated, the rest of our large party jumped into the remaining vehicles.

Our much-anticipated trip was beginning at last! Just thinking about the adventure ahead, already I felt the presence of my ancestors' blood flowing hot through my veins.

I glanced about at my five sisters. As our vehicle began to leave the palace grounds, each of them secured their veils to cover their faces. Yet even under the black cloaks and veils, each sister remained a distinct individual, and I could easily discern one from the other.

Nura had worn eyeglasses for years, and the outline of her glasses was now visible through the fabric of her veil. Tahani's sunglasses were perched on top of her nose, comically on the *outside* of her veil. A red personal stereo rested on top of music-loving Haifa's veil and scarf. I glanced down at the floor and saw brightly coloured Reebok sport shoes peeking out beneath Dunia's cloak. Sara was wearing leather sandals.

Feeling mischievous, and always irritated by the ridiculous custom of veiling, I startled my sisters by crying out, 'Let's make this a new day in our lives! Let's take off our veils and throw them in the dust!' With my arms I reached back to remove my veil.

Sara gave a small scream as she pulled my hands free of my veil.

Looking at me through his rear-view mirror, our Egyptian driver burst out laughing. My feelings regarding the black cloak and veil were well-known to him, and he often seemed to take delight in my unconventional public behaviour.

Nura, the matriarch of the family, lifted her veil and stared sternly at me. 'Sultana! I command you to stop! On this day, you will concentrate on our trip, and not on your veil.'

'Nura, you prove my point,' I teased as I pointed

at her exposed face. 'Even you know that words have little meaning when spoken from behind a veil.'

That was true! The spoken word and facial expression are bonded; one without the other is not taken seriously.

'Sultana!' Nura warned.

Tahani began to giggle at Nura's expression of uneasiness so exposed under her lifted veil. Everyone but Nura joined in her laughter.

'Oh well,' I muttered. 'I suppose it will not hurt me to wear the veil for a few more hours.'

Now understanding that I had been teasing her all along, Nura leaned forward to pinch my arm. I escaped by hiding behind Sara. We began giggling.

I said, 'Do not worry, Nura, Allah obviously wants me to wear this veil that I so detest to the grave.'

Our mood of gaiety continued as our caravan passed several modern towns set in scenic oases of date palms. The plan was that we would set up camp at an area between the Tuwayq Mountains and the Dahna Sands. There was a wadi, a dry river bed, in that area, known as Wadi al Jafi, an old Bedouin route.

The grinding of the gears of our four-wheel-drive vehicles and the lurch of the wheels began to settle as fatigue on my body. I was eager for the journey to end, and our desert adventure to begin. After a few hours of driving, we arrived at an unbroken expanse of sand plains a short distance from Wadi al Jafi. Although there were local villages, settlements and other encampments close by, our tents would be raised in an isolated area.

I liked the spot that Kareem had selected. Solitude and stillness hung over us. Not even birds sang in this treeless place. My sisters, including Nura, and the other women gleefully copied me when I pulled my veil from my face and my *abaaya* from my body.

The removal of our dark outer coverings was not considered improper, since we were now in the familiar arena of our immediate family and servants. It is difficult to hide our faces from those who live on the grounds of our palaces; therefore, out of practical necessity, the males hired by our families soon grow accustomed to seeing the unveiled faces of their employer's wives and daughters.

The wide-open sky and the desert breeze against my skin brought about a sense of well-being. Feeling as free and happy as a child, I laughed as Sara's younger offspring began to chase Tahani's small children. Sand flew from under their bare feet. The little ones too felt the attraction of desert freedom.

With happy anticipation, I then sat in a group with my sisters and our oldest daughters as the men employed by us struggled to erect the black goat-hair tents that would house our families for the next two weeks. We were content as we sipped hot, sugary tea while lounging on carpets spread out on sand hardened in place by the relentless desert winds.

Installing the huge tents was no simple matter, even for those accustomed to this task, and the havoc of toppling tent poles and collapsing roofs caused us to burst into laughter more than once.

Watching the men grapple with the stubborn tents made me particularly grateful for my privileged station in life. Traditionally, every chore associated with the black tent is the sole responsibility of the women. First women shear the goat hair and spin it into yarn, then weave it into fabric for the walls and roofs of the tents. Even then their work is not finished, for from the same yarn, they must also weave floor coverings and other furnishings for the tent interiors, such as wall hangings, carpets and partitions dividing the tent. These 'houses of hair' have been homes to the people of the desert since time eternal.

Although known as black Bedouin tents, the tents are not totally black in colour but are shaded with the various colours present in the wool of the goats. Tent sizes vary, depending on the wealth and importance of the tent owner.

Of course, all of our tents were specially made and much more spacious and elaborate than most poor Bedouins had ever seen. Each tent was comprised of twelve broad strips of black cloth, each seventy-five-feet long. Eight wooden frames held up the tent. Even the smallest of our tents, measuring only sixty feet in length, would be considered enormous by most Bedouin.

We women grew weary of watching the bustling activity long before camp was established. Although we praised the fastest workers, only five tent roofs were upright and taut after several hours of hard work by many men. A large number of tents still waited to be assembled. Surely it would be late into the evening before all our tents were ready.

In our restlessness, we decided to ask Asad to accompany us on a short walk outside the camp area. Soon, with Asad in the lead, a large group of women and children walked gaily out into the desert, even though the sun was still high in the sky and would continue to blaze for several more hours. We turned our bare faces to the sun with much pleasure as we walked behind the scampering children.

Amani's eyes were twinkling with pleasure, for she was coaxing a young baby camel along on our walk. Earlier in the day, when the men unloaded the camels and sheep, Amani had attached herself to this one fawn-coloured baby which now stumbled and cried, swinging its head on its long neck towards Amani. The animal had been taken too young from its mother, so it now recognized a new source of comfort and followed Amani everywhere.

When Amani cooed and began to speak to this camel in a baby voice, I knew that we would not be eating the tender flesh of this particular animal. With its curly coat of soft hair, long limbs, and especially its huge, heavily lashed eyes, the baby camel had stolen all our hearts. My only hope was that Amani would not insist that the camel be housed in our tent.

I sighed heavily as I stared at Amani, wondering how I would ever cure my daughter of her animal follies. Sara touched my shoulder. She and I exchanged a rueful glance. My dear sister understands my every emotion.

The children quickly formed groups and spread out in several directions, promising us that they would stay within sight.

Asad sat down on a small hill and said he would watch us all from that point. He smiled gaily as he held up his high-powered binoculars.

My sisters and I walked on hand-in-hand towards a high rise in the sand. I began to study the infinity of the desert. 'Just think, the totality of our past world once filled this vast emptiness.'

'And not so long ago,' Sara said, as she stooped to pick a yellow desert flower.

'I cannot even imagine the bleak life we women escaped,' Dunia lamented, shuddering at the thought of the bustling work even now going on in the camp.

Nura chuckled as she rolled her eyes. Sara and I exchanged knowing smiles. We had both been truly shocked when we heard that Dunia had agreed to join us on this trip into the desert. Rarely did my sister Dunia venture outside the safety of her palaces. To our surprise, once she was assured there was ample room for her Egyptian massage therapist and Lebanese facial specialist, she finally decided to accompany us.

Sara and I were often annoyed with Dunia's behaviour. Without a doubt, Dunia possesses the ideal personality for a Saudi royal princess. Of the ten daughters born to our mother, none is better at enjoying a life of leisure than Dunia. Her favourite pastime is to make herself as perfect as the imperfections of her face and body will allow. This sister has mastered filling her days with eating, sleeping, undergoing beauty treatments and visiting with her family and friends. Dunia does not read newspapers, magazines or books, nor take any exercise, nor show any interest in the world outside her palace. As the years have passed, I have noticed that Dunia's debilitating fatigue comes earlier and earlier in the day, and her hours of rest have grown longer and longer. I once feared that Dunia might be mentally impaired, but it seems that she is not. Quite simply, nothing stirs Dunia's lazy mind.

Still, Dunia is not a bad person; she has never *hurt* anyone in her life. Yet, as far as I know, Dunia has never *helped* anyone either. Of course, we sisters love her, for no other reason than our beloved mother gave her life. Although Dunia inherited none of our mother's wonderful qualities, she *is* of our blood. We have no choice but to love her.

Nura suddenly stopped and bent forward to scoop up a handful of desert sand. 'Yes. We just barely escaped the harsh life of the nomad.'

Dunia tenderly patted her own face with her hand. 'Nura, you will give me wrinkles of worry with such talk.'

We all laughed loudly. Dunia's lack of passion of any kind, either for or against any subject, in combination with endless facials, massages and special creams, has kept her skin flawless. No wrinkle would dare show on Dunia's face!

Years before, Kareem privately nicknamed this sister, 'The Mummy', saying that nothing of Dunia's years on this earth was written on her face.

Nura grabbed Dunia, hugging her and kissing her loudly on both cheeks. 'Oh! Dunia! You worry about the *possibility* of wrinkles?'

Dunia pursed her lips and forced a smile. As usual, she could think of no fitting reply. Yes, my dear sister's mind must surely be empty, I thought sadly.

From this point, we walked in silence until we reached the top of the rise. Suddenly, the full splendour of the sand dunes of the Dahna Sands came into full view. Grain upon grain of endless sand had formed awesome red mountains of sand; several dunes rose so high that they appeared to touch the edge of the blue sky. I held my breath in wonder at this amazing sight.

My sisters stood quietly, allowing their senses to respond to the ancient sight of red sand that shone like copper in the light of the sun. It was humbling to think that for thousands of years our ancestors have been awed by the beauty of such a panoramic landscape as we were now so fortunate to look up. As we stood enraptured, the absence of human sounds roared in my ears, and I listened carefully to the nothingness. When I strained to look in the distance, though, I thought I saw something moving. I shaded my eyes with my hands. 'Look!' I shouted, as I looked across the sea of sand. 'The dunes are moving!'

The wind was no more than a faint breeze, yet the sand appeared to be rolling towards us. I squinted into the distance. Was this a desert mirage?

Sara lurched backwards in alarm and at the same moment I realized that it was not sand that was in motion, but rather a large group of men on camels moving *across the sand* towards us. These men were strangers, and we were vulnerable and alone, at some distance from our protector Asad, with our faces and hair uncovered! The sounds of piercing cries gave us another shock. Several of the desert travellers had unwound their *ghutras*, their red-and-white checkered head coverings, and were now waving them at us! Obviously, the men were Bedouins who had seen us and were racing their camels in our direction!

Greatly alarmed, my sisters and I yelled for our daughters and young children as we all scrambled back through the sand towards Asad. Tahani screamed in panic when she stumbled over her long dress and pitched forward on the ground. Dunia refused to stop and assist her sister; she ran ahead at exceptional speed and was soon out of sight.

Asad dropped his binoculars as he ran to meet us. When he saw the source of our fear, he entreated us to calm down and swiftly return to the camp. He would remain to greet the desert travellers.

An hour later, my sisters and I were able to laugh about the event. That is, everyone except Dunia. She was still weeping in terror, even though we were now sitting safely inside our spacious tent, protected by our men. Dunia's maid placed one cool cloth after another on the forehead of her terrified mistress, but nothing brought our sister relief. She was convinced that she had narrowly escaped being seized by these men and forced to live out the rest of her life as an unwilling Bedouin wife.

Although it seems strange to us, there are still a few tribes in Arabia who have not capitulated to the urban life. And it is a fact that these desert Arabs have been known to become offended to the point of violence when their offers to buy desirable females are refused. Who can say for certain that these nomads would not have reverted to past customs and simply *stolen* one of us?

In 1979, an American woman whom Sara knows well had narrowly escaped such a fate. While on a day trip into the desert, this woman,

Janet, and her boyfriend, Bill, an American employed by Asad to run one of his many businesses, had come across a Bedouin encampment. Bill, who had lived in Arabia for some time, was fluent in Arabic. When the couple was invited to join the tribe for tea, Bill had been pleased at the rare opportunity to show Janet an authentic Bedouin camp.

But, from the start, this encounter with the Bedouins was unsettling. The tribesmen were captivated by the American woman. Janet was a beautiful woman, with ivory skin, green eyes and wavy, waist-length red hair, and these Bedouin had never seen such a bewitching display of feminine beauty!

Following the second cup of tea, the Bedouin chief grew bold and asked Bill the full price he had paid for his woman. In jest, Bill replied that his woman was *very* costly – a one-hundred camel woman, as a matter of fact. The Bedouin chief shook his head solemnly as he stared at the red-haired beauty. This woman would prove to be very costly indeed! The chief then clapped his hands together and agreed, yes, he would sacrifice the very financial future of his tribe to possess this irresistible temptress. Yes, he, too, would pay one hundred camels for her. Even more. The chief's intense, piercing eyes showed that he *must* have this woman!

To Bill's growing consternation, the chieftain then called for his men to begin gathering one hundred prime camels from his huge herd. When Bill gently rebuffed the generous offer, the amount was increased, once, then twice. When the chief finally understood that the woman was not for sale to him, for *any* number of camels, he quickly moved from a moment of gracious hospitality to a state of offended rage. Were the Bedouin not worthy of such a woman? This was an insult!

The situation deteriorated rapidly, and the frightened couple only barely escaped the incensed mob. They ran to their vehicle and drove away at high speed, but they were chased for a short distance by Bedouins on camels. Who knows what might have happened had they not had a fast vehicle that eventually left the horde of aggrieved and irate Bedouin behind in the dust?

After greeting the Bedouin, Asad had invited them to our camp for tea. He reported that the men who had so frightened us were members of a Bedouin tribe on a hunting party.

We were now waiting for these men to leave so that we could rejoin our husbands. Soon after the aroma of the evening meal began to tease our growling stomachs, we heard the men's loud farewells. After eliciting a promise from our husbands that we would soon visit their camp, the Bedouin men finally left.

Greatly relieved at their departure, I was the first to step through the drawn gap in our tent curtain. My sisters and the other women followed me in the rush from the tent.

Everyone was hungry, so we quickly arranged ourselves in a circle around carpets covered in large white linen cloths that would serve as our table. Although it is the custom in Saudi Arabia for men to eat first, and for women to wait and eat the remains of the meal, it is a custom we do not observe. When the party consists of our family only, all take their meals together. Even the arrogant Ali often eats meals with his wives and children. Therefore, we were all seated cross-legged when our servants brought water jugs for rinsing our hands.

My mouth watered in anticipation of the feast that I knew awaited us. The cooks had been busy preparing our meal since we had first arrived. Their previous disagreements now forgotten, all three cooks proudly stood side-by-side as the procession of food began. Six men carried a huge brass platter that was at least ten feet long. A small camel which had been roasting on a spit all day now lay on a mound of rice on the huge platter. Inside that camel was a lamb, which had been stuffed with chickens. The chickens, in turn, were stuffed with boiled eggs and vegetables. Servants began to place bowls of salads, olives, cheeses and a variety of other dishes before us.

Our eating rituals began in earnest. Kareem uttered the blessing, '*Bismillah*', or 'In the name of Merciful Allah'. In his role as host, Kareem began to insist that Nura's husband, Ahmed, who was the eldest at our family gathering, be the first to sample the food.

Ahmed insisted that, no, he did not deserve such an honour. With mounting fervour, Kareem's voice grew louder and louder as he declared that our family name would be disgraced if Ahmed were not the first to sample the food.

I was hearing but not listening, for I am so accustomed to such ceremonial rituals that I usually think nothing of this delay before eating. But on this occasion I was faint from hunger. Although I said nothing, the idea crossed my mind that we Saudis devote too much time to senseless rites when the outcome is already known. It was a foregone conclusion that Ahmed would *eventually* allow Kareem to convince him to take the first bite.

Kareem and Ahmed went on for so long that I thought I might sneak a meatball from a bowl close to my hand. Just as I eased my hand towards the bowl, Kareem formed a ball of rice in his palm and handed it to Ahmed. My brother-in-law finally relented. He tossed the rice ball into his mouth before tearing off a piece of meat from the carcass of the camel and stuffing his mouth.

This was the signal that the feast could now begin. Bowls were passed from hand to hand, while other eager hands reached towards the large platter. Everyone was so hungry that this was a rare occasion when no conversation interrupted our eating.

After we had consumed all we wanted of the main course, the servants began to bring out tray after tray of sweets made of cream, nuts and honey. Although our stomachs were full, everyone sampled the delicious sweets.

Voices rose with the thanksgiving of '*Alhamdulilah*', or 'Thanks be to God'. Finally, silver bowls filled with rose water were brought out for everyone to wash their hands and mouths. Our meal was finished.

Kareem suggested, 'Everyone, come, let us sit upon the ground by the campfire.'

With the disappearance of the sun, the evening air of the desert was now chilly, so we were happy to congregate around the glowing embers of the big fire. Even the smallest children joined us. We embarked on the custom of sharing our history, a favourite activity of all family gatherings.

As the servants began to serve us coffee and tea, and lemonade for the younger children, various family members began to tell exciting stories in verse of caravan life and tribal war.

In the past, Arabs and Bedouins had frequently raided each other. Such vicious attacks were considered an honourable way to support one's tribe. No warriors were feared more than Al Sa'ud warriors, for they mercilessly slaughtered their enemies, bragging that in their raids they never left a single warrior alive. Those considered innocent – women, children and the elderly – found themselves distributed among the victorious.

Stirred by these stories, the older men in our family obviously felt the draw of our past, for when Ahmed jumped to his feet, calling out for the servants to bring him his sword, our husbands joined him. Soon our party was rewarded with the men's dancing of the *ardha*, a version of an Arab war dance.

I smiled broadly as I watched Kareem and the other men hopping about and chanting, brandishing their swords in extravagant movements. Brother Ali began to sword-joust with Asad, but soon gave way, red-faced and flustered. Although Ali is much larger than the trim Asad, over the years Ali's flesh has turned to fat, while the highly disciplined Asad has retained his healthy muscle.

After much gaiety, our men, breathing hard, returned to sit around the campfire. They lifted water jugs up into the air and aimed the spouts towards their mouths. Skilfully, they directed the flow of the water directly into their throats without splashing a single drop on their lips.

When Tahani began to tell a Bedouin love story, Ali interrupted her, scoffing at such sentiments. Much to my dismay, Tahani fell silent immediately.

Ali looked towards the youngest children, sternly saying, 'These tales of love will bend your minds in the wrong direction. The most important lesson of all is to be learned from the story I am about to tell you.'

I exchanged a glance with Sara, but remembering my promise to Kareem that I would not fight with my brother while on this trip, I attempted to feign interest.

Even surrounded by so many women of his own family, my brother could not control his deep bias against women. He had the nerve to tell the tale of a young Bedouin man, who, after being viciously attacked by members of a rival tribe, and grievously wounded, had his life saved by a woman who was a stranger to him. That young man had been so revolted to discover an unknown woman's hands on his body that he had spat in the woman's face, and called out for her to be stoned! Ali looked at his young sons and nephews, and, confident in his exalted role as a wise elder, he told the impressionable young men and boys that it was better to *die* at the hands of male attackers than to be *saved* by a strange woman!

My mouth fell open. To keep from speaking up, I was forced to hold my tongue between my teeth.

Ali's story met with disapproval from every corner, but everyone was far more polite than Ali deserved, and, to my disappointment, no furore of criticism fell on his ears.

The female faces were still sullen when Kareem cleared his throat and offered a final story. My heart went out to my husband, for it was apparent to me that he wanted our young children to retire to sleep with other ideas in their minds than those from Ali's perverse tale.

Kareem directed his attention to the children and young adults. 'Dear children, the most desirable trait any person can claim is generosity and hospitality. And, it is my pleasure to tell you about an Arab man who was the most generous man ever to live.'

My husband then told a popular Bedouin story that touches the heart of every Arab, for nothing impresses us more than stories of great generosity.

'It is said that all great men are born in small tents. And this was the case with Sheik Hatim. He was born in a small tent, but through hard work raised himself to be one of the richest sheiks who pastured their herds in the great desert.

'This sheik's name was in every man's mouth, not because of his wealth, but due to that great Arab virtue generosity, which he practised more faithfully than any man alive. Sheik Hatim gave to all who asked, and never questioned the need of anyone. He refused no-one's request, not even his enemies. Once four hundred starving men, women and children travelled from drought-scorched hills to this sheik's tent. What did he do? He killed and roasted fifty camels to supply them with meat.

'The Sultan of Roum, hearing about this sheik, was certain that his generosity was a pretence, that it was a way of advertising himself and the things he had for sale. The Sultan decided to send his men to ask Sheik Hatim for his most prized possession, a precious stallion known throughout the land, to see if the sheik was as generous as people said.

'This stallion, named Duldul, was the finest horse in all of Arabia. He had been raised with Hatim's children, and had shared in all the joys and sorrows of Hatim's household. The horse was so loved that he had never known the touch of a whip or heard an unkind word.

'Well, the Sultan's men got lost along the way in a great storm, and when they arrived, they were half-starved and almost dead. They were surprised to see only three small tents, and no herds of animals, although Sheik Hatim met them on his beloved steed, Duldul.

'The Sultan's men saw plainly that the sheik was not expecting guests, yet he greeted them with warmth and great hospitality. Seeing his guests in such pitiful condition, the sheik declared that he would prepare a feast.

'After witnessing the bare grazing land, those men were surprised when they later sat down to a meal of delicious meat, which had been broiled, and roasted, and made into soups and savoury dishes. The hungry men declared that they had never been fed so royally.

'The Sultan's men then became ashamed of their errand, and told the sheik that they had been sent by the Sultan of Roum to test his generosity by asking for the stallion Duldul.

'Sheik Hatim sat as though he had been stunned by a heavy blow. His face became deathly white before he said, "Ah, friends, if you had only made your errand known in the beginning. You could not have fathomed my circumstances. I was not prepared for guests, for we arrived at this spot only two days ago. We have been waiting for our household and flocks, but a great rain fell and flash torrents prevented them from reaching us. When you arrived, exhausted and hungry, what was I to do? There was no meat in my tent – and no goats or sheep within a day's journey. Could I fail to provide hospitality? I could not bear the thought of hungry men in my tent. And so my prized horse, Duldul, that matchless steed who knew my every wish and obeyed my every word – what else could I do?"

'Tears were flowing down the sheik's face when he said, "Now, go and tell your disbelieving Sultan Roum that in my extremity, I *cooked* and served the beautiful and obedient Duldul for your suppers." '

Kareem now smiled at the youngest children, who were wide-eyed at the thought of such hospitality. 'Now children, know that you have heard the story of a true Arab – the best Arab – a man whose generosity is never questioned.'

Kareem's tale had us all smiling and in a good humour as the party began to break up and move towards the individual tents.

But when Ali passed by me, his arrogant look still irritated me. When my brother offered his cheek to me for a goodnight kiss, I stiffened. Out of the corner of my eye, I saw Kareem watching me.

I smiled, then stood on my tiptoes.

Ali leaned closer.

My lips brushed teasingly past his cheek before I

whispered a favoured Bedouin curse into Ali's ear, 'May *every* camel in your herd *go lame*, Ali.'

While Kareem looked at me with loving approval, Ali stared at me in startled bewilderment. He was still revelling in his role as a wise man, and could not fathom the reason for my words of disdain.

I smiled triumphantly as I made my way to our tent.

Our tent had been readied earlier in the day according to Kareem's instructions. It was divided into five parts. With velvet curtains serving as partitions, the largest room was arranged for entertaining and eating, two rooms were for sleeping, and two more rooms served as bathrooms. Kareem and I would share one bedroom and bath, and our daughters the other.

I walked through the largest room where small, custom-made sofas as well as peach and beige silk cushions lined two walls. Persian carpets covered the sandy floor of the desert. Camel saddles decorated with gold and silver fringes, to be used later by our men while on desert outings, lined a third wall. Banners, swords and the Saudi flag added to the array of decorations.

The cosy contours of the bedrooms had been furnished with unique pieces of beautiful furniture. Our beds were crowned with lightweight canopies, and draped with a sheer fabric that would screen our bodies from the desert dust and insects.

My maid had already laid out my sleeping gown, and after washing my face and cleaning my teeth, I slipped out of my dress. I sighed with contentment as I stretched across my side of the bed. This day in my life had been more agreeable than most. I was asleep within moments, and never even heard Kareem when he came into the room.

Swirling Sands

The following days were most pleasant for the whole family. Our men mounted their camels and hunted desert wildlife while our children played endless games with their cousins. The women enjoyed long walks around the camp, admiring the scenic vistas and sharing many happy memories of our childhood.

Three days into our trip, our husbands suggested that we visit the camp of the Bedouin tribe whose men had so startled us on our first day. We women were eager to go, for every city Arab remains forever curious about the Bedouin.

All the women except Dunia, that is. Dunia flatly refused the invitation, claiming that her frail temperament simply could not survive the shock of visiting a dirty Bedouin camp, so she stayed behind with our female servants and the children.

People unfamiliar with Arabia believe all Arabs are Bedouin; actually, city Arabs and desert Bedouin Arabs have rarely co-existed peacefully, and even today a pervasive and continuing conflict exists between them. City Arabs mock the Bedouin as simple-minded fools while Bedouins revile city Arabs as amoral sinners. In the not too distant past, the 'wild Bedu' would stuff their nostrils with cloth when it was necessary for them to come into the city, to avoid being polluted by the odour of city Arabs.

Still, Bedouins always extend a warm reception to visitors to their camps, even though this hospitality is often short-lived.

I had been in several Bedouin camps during my youth, and now I was interested to discover if the years in between had brought any improvement to their grim lives. I recalled that the Bedouin I had seen had been packed into tents filled with their own garbage.

The life of the Bedouin begins with a high risk of infant mortality. Those children who survive infancy run barefoot, unschooled and unwashed through the camps. And, the women! I could scarcely think of them without an involuntary wince. Certainly, in every class of Saudi Arabian life, women are looked down upon as naturally and irrevocably inferior to men, but life for Bedouin women is worse by any measure, for they do not have the necessary wealth to relieve their harsh lives. Bedouin women are terribly burdened by hard physical labour. Besides waiting on their husbands, and taking care of many children, their nomadic responsibilities include the setting up and dismantling of the camp.

These thoughts were in my mind as we endured our bumpy ride over the desert floor. Thankfully, the distance we drove was no more than fifteen kilometres. Soon the curling smoke of a campfire could be seen in the distance. But the men of the camp had seen the dust from our vehicles long before we saw their campfire. More than twenty men had mounted their camels and were now waiting a short distance from the entrance of their tent settlement.

One particular Bedouin caught my eye. He was a robust man of middle age, with chiselled features and dominating black eyes. With his long black cloak flowing behind him he was regal, as was his magnificent mount, a strong, young female camel. His Bedouin gaze was piercing and directed towards us with unquestioning self-confidence. No smile came to his lips at the sight of strange visitors, although I found it amusing that the lips of his camel seemed permanently carved into a smile.

With a strutting kind of dignity, he rode around our vehicles more than once, as though inspecting us. I knew without asking that this man was the chief of his village. The Bedouin are proud, and not in awe of any man, not even men of the royal family. He would show us all that our welcome depended upon his approval.

When Ahmed stuck his head out of the window of the vehicle, the chief, who said his name was Sheik Fahd, finally stretched his face in a welcoming smile. With a voice like thunder, he greeted us with the hope of Allah's blessing. With a flourish of both hands, he pointed the way to his village.

At this sign, the other Bedouins began to shout their welcome. They rode cheerfully alongside our vehicles as we slowly made our way to the camp.

When Sheik Fahd called out that he had honoured guests, the Bedouin settlement instantly came to life. Veiled women with their arms filled with infants, and many poorly dressed young children, emerged from the row of sloping tents.

The moment I stepped out of our jeep, I was struck by the strong odour in the air. My nose twitched with the stench of close-living animals and blood-soaked slaughter pits. I stepped daintily, for the ground was polluted with animal droppings. This was a village cleaned only by the rains, and no rain had fallen for a long time. I told myself that each step I took was a step backwards in time.

More than ten women dressed in brightly coloured dresses and covered with the Bedouin veil walked towards us. It is customary for Bedouin women to leave their eyes uncovered, while the tradition of city Arab women is to conceal the entire face. When these women welcomed us, all their energies flowed out through their dark and vivid eyes.

Our husbands went off with the men to the sheik's tent to enjoy tea, while my sisters and I followed the camp women. The tallest of the women, who was dressed in a brightly coloured blue dress covered in gold embroidery was named Faten, and she quickly let us know that she was the favourite of the sheik's four wives. Her eyes flashed with pride as she led us towards her personal tent.

As decreed by the Koran, this Bedouin chief apparently provided each of his wives with her own tent, in the same manner that city Arabs build individual villas or palaces for each wife.

As we were escorted inside, Faten said with a flourish, 'As the most favoured wife of Sheik Fahd, I welcome you to my tent.'

As we entered the flapping goat-hair door of Faten's tent, I looked around with undisguised interest. The interior was dark and stuffy, just as I remembered the Bedouin tents of my childhood. In the centre of the room there was a coffee hearth surrounded by piles of white ashes from previous fires. Numerous gaudy tints caught my eyes. Cushions of various orange, blue and red hues were piled against mattresses, and brightly coloured quilts, pots and pans, food items and folded clothes were heaped up everywhere.

Everything appeared unclean, and the tent carried the foul aroma of disease. Saddest of all was the sight of the small children. The cries of several fussy babies filled the room, and shy, grubby toddlers peeked around from behind their mothers. I watched sadly as one unhappy little boy, who looked to be four or five years old, used his hands to pull himself along the floor. When one of the women saw that his pitiful crippled condition drew my attention, she volunteered the information that, when he was only an infant, his mother had accidentally dropped him from a camel.

I tried to take him in my arms, but he began to scream with fear. One of the women, who I assumed was his mother, slapped his shrunken legs until he dragged himself to a corner of the tent where he lay whimpering.

I was brokenhearted at this child's plight. Unlike people of other cultures, Arabs, and in particular Bedouin Arabs, are uncaring about their handicapped. While healthy children are considered wealth and prestige for a family, an unhealthy child is a dreaded shame. It was doubtful that this child would ever receive medical attention. The little boy would likely live out his miserably short life crippled, unloved and undernourished.

I desperately wanted to scoop the little boy up and take him away with me, but such a reaction is unheard of in my country. In such a case as neglect, children are *never* taken away from their families, no matter what the circumstances.

When one of the women roughly nudged my arm, I accepted the tea cup offered me. It was crusted with the filth of much previous use. A second woman, with the scarred hands of a woman who had raised many tents, poured hot tea into my cup. There was nothing to do but to drink from this cup, otherwise our hostess would be gravely offended.

Once she was satisfied that her guests had been served, Faten removed her veil. She was proud to show us that she was, indeed, very pretty, and very young, no more than eighteen or nineteen years of age, close to Maha's age.

The other Bedouin women removed their veils, too. These women looked much older and more worn-out than Faten. It was no wonder that she was the favourite wife, for she had not yet been ravaged by repeated childbirth and the harsh desert life.

Faten pranced before us as she showed off the various trinkets that she said were special gifts from the sheik. 'He no longer visits his other wives,' she said with a broad grin as she pointed out three other Bedouin women in attendance. The three women exchanged subtle looks of irritation, while my sisters and I sat in silent unease. When one of the older women insisted that my sisters and I also remove our veils, we did so.

Faten gawked in surprise at Sara's beauty.

Obviously, she was accustomed to being the village celebrity, but no woman could match Sara's breathtaking loveliness. If my dear sister lived in a country where women were not forced to cover their faces, she would be famous for her magnificent beauty.

The other women fluttered around Sara and began to touch her face and hair. One of them told Faten that if Sheik Fahd were ever to see such a one as Sara, that he was sure to abandon her bed in frustration. The other three wives of the sheik quickly agreed.

The visibly spoiled Faten became jealous and began to command the other women to retrieve this item or that item. Her voice was far too impolite and loud, and as a token of resistance, the women pretended not to understand her instructions.

The words exchanged became so harsh and the looks so fierce that I feared we were about to witness an altercation between these ill-mannered women. This display made me reflect on what would have been the reality of my own life had our ancestors not abandoned the desert for the city. In the Bedouin culture, a woman's status depends only on her youth, beauty and ability to produce sons. Certainly, a Bedouin woman of my age who had suffered the loss of a breast and the ability to bear children would be cast aside by her husband. Undoubtedly, I would have become the servant of an insensitive beauty such as Faten!

For the first time in a long time, I acknowledged that Saudi Arabians are taking some small progressive steps towards improving the lives of Saudi women. I felt a rare moment of gratitude for my current status.

When an embarrassed Sara threatened to veil her face again if she was not left alone, the women cried out that they would sit quietly for the pleasure of looking at Allah's most perfect creation.

Faten could take no more! Her lip curled in anger as she glared at Sara, and cursed her. 'A pox on you! May Allah disfigure your face!'

We were all speechless with shock at this uncivilized behaviour.

In dignified silence, Sara rose to leave. Faten mistook Sara's movement as a challenge. Her wide-set eyes grew wild, her nostrils flared, and she advanced towards my gentle sister with the clear intent of violence! Frightened, Sara froze in place, her hand poised at her throat.

Since Sara's unfortunate first marriage, when she was brutalized at the hands of a cruel husband, everyone in our family is determined to offer Sara unconditional physical protection. Nura moved forward to shield Sara, but she was not as fast as her youngest sister.

I stepped in front of Sara just as Faten's hand reached out for her. I felt a sharp tug on my face. The crazy Bedouin woman had twisted my nose!

I had once heard my father say that, 'He that does not make a Bedouin fear him, will soon fear the Bedouin.' Quite obviously, this woman would understand nothing but force. As Faten reached out to twist my nose once more, I gave a loud cry as I leapt towards her. It has been years since I was involved in any kind of physical altercation, but my years of childhood fighting with the much larger Ali had taught me to make my moves swift and certain. I am too small to long outlast a big woman like Faten. I moved quickly to get a stranglehold on her neck, forcing her backwards onto the foor. I tripped on my long skirt and fell on top of my opponent.

The other Bedouin women obviously hated Faten, for they did nothing to help her; rather, they laughed and cheered *me* on.

One woman shouted, 'Oh, Princess! Poke out her eyes!'

Another encouraged me, 'Twist her neck!'

My sisters became hysterical with fear that the vicious Faten would get the best of their baby sister. Their screams resonated through the small tent.

Faten managed to scrape a handful of sand from the floor, and tossed it into my face.

Blinded, I pulled Faten's hair until her hands clawed the air as she pleaded for Allah's mercy.

For good measure I pounded her head twice on the hard earth, then rose to my feet. While brushing off my skirt, I offered the greatest insult I could think of. 'This is how you welcome your guests?'

I knew that the true Bedouin tradition treats guests with great respect. Even a mortal enemy is permitted three days of grace after departing the boundaries of a Bedouin tent.

Faten's face had reddened with each word I spoke, but she made no further advance towards me. The Bedouin women began to laugh hysterically at Faten's defeat.

Nura and Tahani rushed to brush the sand from my face and hair.

Tahani cried out, 'Sultana! Did she hurt you?'

I laughed, 'No.' When my eyes locked with Faten's eyes in mutual hatred, I flung her my final insult. 'This Bedouin fights like a small child.'

Quickly fastening our veils over our faces, the three of us followed Sara and Haifa as they hurried out of the tent.

Meanwhile, the men had heard the commotion, and spilled out of Fahd's tent, looking around in confused concern. As we approached our husbands, and were about to explain the situation, a wild scream exploded from behind us.

What was happening, now? I wondered.

I turned to see the sands swirling from the force of Faten's running footsteps. The crazy Bedouin grabbed two fistfuls of sand and rushed towards me. Before I could move, she had thrown the sand on my head, screaming, 'May Allah pour all his punishments upon your head!'

Words failed the men. They were struck dumb at Faten's outrageous gesture of contempt. My blood ran cold at her curse, but I was dignified and silent as I leaned forward and brushed the sand from my head and veil. Let Faten appear the villain.

With great satisfaction, one of the older Bedouin women explained to Sheik Fahd that his new bride had physically assaulted his guests.

'Sultana!' Kareem rushed towards me. 'Are you hurt?'

The sheik sprinted after Faten, who was now running away. We heard him shouting, 'You stupid woman! You dishonour my tent!'

Faten was sure to get a good thrashing by her

husband, but here was a woman who deserved a beating, I reasoned.

Nura urged our men to take us away from what was, for us, a primitive and frightening place, and they quickly complied.

When everyone heard the full story, I was praised as a heroine. Sara is the most beloved member of our entire family, and even Kareem understood that I had no option but to defend her. Asad was so shaken at the thought that a crazed Bedouin woman nearly attacked his beloved, that he told Sara he was going to buy me the most expensive piece of jewelry available in Riyadh, as a gift of thanks. Even Ali looked upon my act with great pride, and told everyone that would listen that he was the one who had taught me my fighting skills, which I had to agree was true. For the next few days, talk of my victorious fight with Faten kept our camp in a high state of excitement.

When Sheik Fahd offered an apology in the form of ten female Batiniyah camels, we knew that Faten's behaviour was indeed a source of great shame to that proud Bedouin chief. Batiniyah camels are from Oman, and are considered one of the best species of camels. The ten camels were of high quality, for they all had small heads, wide foreheads, large eyes, small nostrils and long ears.

A Bedouin tribe's wealth is measured by the size and quality of its camel herd, and ten Batiniyah camels are extremely costly. Suspecting that they represented the best of Sheik Fahd's herd, Kareem had no wish to accept this expensive gift. Still, he could not decline, for his refusal would have offended Sheik Fahd deeply. So, the Batiniyah beauties joined our own herd.

After such a melodrama, we attempted to enjoy the remaining days of our desert trip with more quiet pursuits.

Buried While Still Alive

Several mornings before we were to return to Riyadh, I was rudely awakened by Maha.

'Mother,' she screamed, 'come quickly. Uncle Ali is dying.'

Groggy from sleep, I questioned, 'What are you saying, child?'

'Uncle Ali has been bitten by a poisonous snake! By now, he has drawn his last breath!'

'Allah! No!'

My maid stood by with one of my full cotton dresses, which she flung over my nightgown. I slipped into a spare pair of Kareem's sandals that were at the doorway of the tent, and I ran with Maha to Ali's tent.

A large crowd of our servants and employees had gathered outside the tent. As Maha and I worked our way through the crowd, I overheard their excited talk. One of the Filipinos was saying, 'He was walking only a few steps from the camp, when out of nowhere, a huge snake appeared and bit him on the hand!'

'Those snakes can fly like a bird,' one of our Egyptian employees claimed excitedly.

Another Sudanese man reported, 'Even a big

man cannot survive the bite of the *yaym*!'

With those words I groaned. The *yaym*! If not already dead, Ali was sure to die. I knew that the venom of that snake was more deadly than the strongest poison. The *yaym*, from the cobra family, is one of three venomous species in Arabia, and the rarest. Since it is seldom seen, there are few accounts of its causing a death.

Although my brother has made it easy for me to dislike and, at times even hate him, I have never wished him dead. But I have always had strong desire for Ali to *change* his evil ways. Should Ali die on this day, he would die a wicked sinner. Such a thought was disturbing to my mind, for I knew that this would greatly sadden my mother's spirit.

When I tore through the opening in the tent, my body sagged at the sight that greeted me. Ali was lying motionless on a mattress on the floor, surrounded by his wives, who seemed to be already in mourning. He *is* dead, I thought, as I gave a tortured scream.

Kareem rushed to my side. 'Sultana!'

I leaned against Kareem's broad chest and began to weep.

'Sultana, Ali has been asking for you,' Kareem told me.

'He is still with the living?' I asked in amazement.

'He is – but you must be brave. It seems his time has come.'

I looked around the room and saw that the crisis had spurred our family into a frenzy of activity. Nura, Sara and Haifa were busy chopping the leaves of the *ramram* plant. Once ground, this substance would be made into a tea, which Bedouins routinely use as an antidote for the poison of venomous snakes. Yet, I knew that if Allah had determined this particular day for Ali's passing, nothing my sisters could do would change his fate. All Muslims believe that each person's fate is determined at the beginning of time, and that no mortal man has the capability to change or interfere with God's plan.

Ali cried out, 'Oh Allah, save me, I beg you!'

Kareem led me to my brother's side. My heart seemed to plunge when I saw that Ali was sweating profusely, and that his lips had turned blue. Indeed, it appeared that my brother had only moments left to live.

Ali's wives moved aside, and so I knelt down by Ali's side.

'Ali,' I whispered. 'It is your sister, Sultana.'

At first there was no response. Instead, Ali struggled to breathe.

I squeezed his cold hands.

My brother turned his head and opened his eyes, looking directly into my face. His own expression was one of great sorrow. 'Sultana?'

'Yes?' I braced myself for an emotional moment. Surely Ali was now going to apologize for his life's unsavoury deeds. How could he die without first acknowledging, and then expressing regret for, the enormous pain he had caused me and other women?

Just then, Nura came rushing to Ali's side. 'Here,' she said in an urgent tone. 'Ali, open your mouth and swallow this.' Nura was holding a cup of the tea made from the *ramram* plant. She held the cup to Ali's lips.

As Ali drank the tea, Nura whispered to him consolingly, telling him that he must try very hard to live.

'Yes, I will try, Nura,' Ali said determinedly. 'I will try.'

I, too, hoped that Ali would not die. Possibly such a fright would make him become a better father and husband, I reasoned.

I waited at Ali's side. After a short time, he looked directly at me. He whispered, 'Sultana, is it you?'

'Yes, Ali.'

'Sultana, for sure, I will be dead within moments.'

I sighed deeply, not wanting to argue with his words, should Ali's death on this day be God's will. But when I looked closely at him, I saw that his lips were not quite as blue as before. Perhaps the antidote was working.

Ali waited to see if I had anything else to say. When I remained silent, he spoke once more. 'Sultana. Since I am on the way to the grave, I thought perhaps you might have something important to say to me.'

Confused, I sputtered, 'Well, Ali, I wish Allah's kindness and blessings on you.'

'Oh?' Ali's face fell in disappointment.

What did my brother want from me?

Haltingly, Ali spoke once more. 'Sultana, I thought perhaps you would wish to apologize to me.'

In my surprise, my voice rose higher than I intended. '*Apologize?*'

Ali looked positively stricken at my response, yet by the sound of his voice, I could tell that he was gaining strength. 'Yes,' he said, 'Sultana, you should apologize for your wicked behaviour. You have tormented me for all of my life.'

So! Ali's renewed strength had brought back his arrogance! I was so shocked at this unexpected turn that I began to stammer once again, 'I have *nothing* to apologize about, Ali! In truth, I was waiting to hear *your* apology!'

Ali gave me a long, stony look. Finally, he whispered, 'I have done no harm. I have been an excellent father to my children, a good husband to my wives, an obedient son to my father, and a supportive brother to my sisters. What is there to apologize for?'

I could only stare at my brother in despair. Did he truly believe the words he spoke? I quickly decided that my brother was actually helpless when it came to recognizing his own evil! Quite simply, Ali did not have the capacity to think like a *normal* human being. Ali *truly* believed that it was *I* who was the wicked sinner!

At that moment, I had to curb my tongue or I would have cursed Ali. Although driven by a fierce passion, I did not wish to be haunted by deep regrets. And regret it I would if my brother died with my curses ringing in his ears.

Still, it was difficult to hold back every word. I released my hand from Ali's hand and then patted his face. 'May Allah give you the two greatest blessings, Ali.'

Ali smiled. 'Thank you, Sultana.' He then frowned slightly, 'What two blessings do you wish me?'

I smiled back. 'I pray for Allah to crown you with good health, but most importantly, Ali, I pray for Allah to provide you with self awareness of your wickedness.'

Ali's jaw slackened in surprise.

I then left his side without waiting for his response. For the first time in my life, my brother's thoughts and behaviour no longer held sway over me. The strong chain of hate linking us had been for ever severed. I no longer hated Ali; indeed, I felt a rush of sympathy for him.

With other members of my family, I waited in Ali's tent to see what the day might bring. We watched as Ali thrashed and moaned, calling out for a quick delivery from his pain. There were moments we believed that he would die any minute, and other times when it appeared that he would live to see another sunrise.

The snake that had bitten Ali was cornered and captured by several of our employees. The happy discovery was made that the snake was not after all a *yaym*, as feared, but a *hayyah*, or sand viper. The *hayyah* is poisonous, too, but its venom is not nearly as deadly as that of the *yaym*. Most who are bitten by the *hayyah* do survive, although the experience is frightening and painful.

Everyone rejoiced in the knowledge that Ali, once given up as dead, would survive. Asad comforted Ali with the news, then said, 'Thanks be to God, Ali, for your sisters who prepared the antidote.'

That was true, the antidote had obviously diminished Ali's pain and quickened his recovery. But with cool indifference, Ali dismissed his sisters' efforts.

'No, Asad,' he said, 'it was just not my time. Remember the wise saying that until my day comes, no-one can harm me, when my day comes, no-one can save me.' Ali smiled. 'My sisters had nothing to do with the ending of this day.'

Even Ali's wives exchanged incredulous looks at these words. Still, in view of his near death, his family was in a charitable mood, and no-one reprimanded him.

Before leaving his tent, each of us filed by Ali's bedside and wished him a speedy recovery. When it was my turn, he looked at me and sneered. 'Ah, Sultana, I knew that God would not take such a man as me from this beautiful world while leaving such a sinner as you to enjoy his blessings.'

I smiled sadly at Ali. And, although he and I embraced, I understood that in my brother's eyes, he and I remained enemies.

With Kareem by my side, I returned exhausted to our own tent. Kareem slept easily all through the night, but my sleep was not so peaceful. Mother returned to me in the night, in the form of endless dreams. She kept repeating the same message: that my earthly life was not bringing me the happiness and fulfilment that *was* attainable. I did not awaken until the sound of the early morning prayers drifted into our tent.

My dreams had been so real that the years in between Mother's death and the present time had vanished. And so, I looked expectantly around the room, fully believing that my mother would be there, in the flesh, waiting with soft words to ease her youngest child into another day.

Then I remembered that Mother had been dead for more years than I had even known her. I was only sixteen years old when she died, and I had now lived twenty-four long years without a mother's embrace. That thought so depressed me that I rose from bed, dressed quickly, and left the tent without telling anyone where I was going.

With tears of despair streaming down my face, I walked alone into the desert.

What was it that my mother wanted from me? How could I be what she thought I should be? Where had I failed? What changes could I make in my life?

My mind was so tortured that I failed to see the sky lighten as the sun began to rise over the desert. I did not even see Sara approaching until she sat down by my side.

Sara touched my arm, 'Sultana?'

The expression in my eyes appeared to distress Sara. She asked me, 'Dearest love, are you all right?'

Weeping, I threw myself in my sister's arms.

'You must tell me, Sultana. Whatever is the matter?'

I choked on my sobs as I whispered, 'I have always drawn my life as I wished to see it, Sara. But, now, I know that I have lived a useless life. Mother has told me so.'

Sara studied my face carefully, then said, 'Your life has not been useless, Sultana. You have protected your children. You have made Kareem a happy man. And, you have undergone great personal danger to alert the world to our women's plight.'

'Not enough . . . not enough . . .' I muttered tearfully. 'Mother keeps telling me that I should do more.'

Sara sat without speaking for a long time. At

length, after long moments of quiet reflection, she said, 'Sultana, few of us do *enough*. I finally know that now.'

I looked with new interest at Sara. Had she been dreaming of Mother, too?

'What do you mean?' I asked.

Sara sighed deeply, before retrieving a much-folded piece of paper from the pocket of the jacket she was wearing over her dress.

Her words were slow and soft. 'It is so easy to be a coward in Saudi Arabia. There is so much to lose.'

Sara looked so empty and sad. Whatever was she speaking about?

'Sultana, I now realize that I should have moved the very earth to help Munira. Together, with our other sisters, we could have succeeded in helping that poor girl to escape to another country.'

I gasped. Had something happened to Munira? Was she dead?

Sara handed me the paper in her hands. 'I just found this last evening.' Sara's voice lowered, 'I am brokenhearted with remorse.'

I opened up the paper and saw that small, precise handwriting filled the page.

Sara explained. 'Some weeks ago, I lent Munira one of my books. The day Munira returned the book, I was packing for this trip. Thinking that I might reread this book while on the trip, I packed it with my luggage. I could not sleep last night, so I opened the pages of the book, and this is what I discovered.'

Sara's eyes were red and wet with tears.

She flicked her finger on the page. 'Read what Munira has to say, Sultana.'

Convinced that I was about to read a suicide note, my hands began to shake so much that I could barely focus my eyes on the moving page. Sara helped me to hold the page firm.

What Munira had written was a poem.

Buried Alive

I have lived and known what it is to smile
I have lived the life of a young girl with hopeful
  promise
I have lived the life of a young girl who felt the
  warmth of womanhood
I have lived the feeling of longing for the love of
  a good man
I have lived the life of a woman whose promise
  was cut short
I have lived the life of one whose dreams were
  dashed
I have lived knowing tremendous fear for every
  man
I have lived through the fears raised by the
  spectre of an evil coupling
I have lived to see the devil in the guise of a
  man, ruling my every action
I have lived as a beggar to this man, pleading
  with him to leave me alone
I have lived to witness my husband have the
  pleasure of being a man
I have lived to be ravished by the man to whom
  I was given
I have lived only to endure nightly rapes
I have lived to be buried while still alive

I have lived to wonder why those who claim to
  love me, helped to bury me
I have lived through all of these things, and I am
  not yet twenty-five years old

We were both speechless with unbearable pain; my sister and I could only stare at each other. Without saying a single word to Sara, I knew that no matter the consequences, I must now do more to bring change to the lives of women, who, like Munira, were in danger of being buried before they were dead.

I returned with my sister to the camp, knowing that my life was now for ever changed. There was no turning back.

Sultana's Circle

I once read that for every gift that Allah grants His children, He also attaches an equal challenge. I believe this to be true, for I have never heard about, or even read about, a single human life that encompasses only perfection and happiness. Certainly my own character is riddled with imperfections, and because of these flaws I have faced many sorrows.

Although I have been the beneficiary of numerous blessings, I have also been presented with many obstacles. In choosing my parents, God linked a cruel father with a loving mother. He gave me wonderful years with my mother, and then took her from me when I was still of a tender age. He granted me the lofty status of princess in a royal kingdom, yet that elevated status would be of little value in a land traditionally hostile to females.

For some years now, I have seen my life spread out before me as though it were already written. I do not like what I know will come to be: my wealth will multiply and my possessions will increase, but at the same time my happiness and contentment will decrease. An uneasiness with the pattern of my daily life created a problem with alcohol that led me into a listless life where I foolishly squandered my prospects for achieving my life-long goal of assisting women in need. The fact that these handicaps were self-imposed undermined my feelings of worthiness. The Sultana of an earlier time, who once dreamed of a glorious destiny, had become an apathetic soul, miserable and lost.

Miraculously, I was given this new understanding that the pattern of my life must now change: my beloved mother's coming to me in dreams; the effect of Munira's plaintive poem; even my brother Ali's near-death experience; each contributed to my new perspective. I will always believe that God Himself masterfully arranged these happenings with the clear purpose of bringing forth the magical metamorphosis that I experienced that day in the desert. For one who believes in the power of Almighty God, there can be no other explanation.

Although in that instant my life became even more complicated, I have no regrets. Had my dramatic transition *not* occurred, I know that I would have remained mired in a restless unhappiness. More importantly, a young Pakistani woman by the name of Veena would have continued to live in brutal sexual bondage.

'Never again,' I told Sara as we walked back into camp. 'Never again will I remain silent in the face of cruelty and maltreatment to *any* woman.'

Sara nodded grimly. She understood. Just at that moment I saw Dunia's youngest son, Shadi, step out from a vehicle and begin to greet his uncles and cousins with great enthusiasm.

'Shadi has arrived,' Sara softly murmured.

'Dunia is sure to be happy,' I replied with a smile.

Shadi is a tall, heavily built young man of twenty who does not present a particularly attractive appearance. Any personal knowledge I had of this nephew was slight, though, for we saw each other only at large family events. I now vaguely recalled Dunia's mentioning earlier that Shadi would be late in joining his family on this desert journey. Already Dunia had been proud to announce that Shadi was her most brilliant son, and that his expertise in business dealings far surpassed every other young man in the Al Sa'ud family. In fact, Dunia smugly confided to all who would listen, Shadi owned several joint business interests in Pakistan, and was just coming back from a trip to that country to purchase even more businesses. My sisters and I had not taken personal offence at thoughtless words, even though they were an insult to our own beloved sons.

At that moment, Sara and I did not go forward to greet Shadi since he was already surrounded by his uncles and eager young male cousins. We would welcome the young man later, we decided, as we walked towards our own tents.

I was not particularly surprised to see a young woman in Pakistani clothes sitting in the back seat of Shadi's vehicle; our men frequently drive our female servants from one place to another. I assumed the young woman was one of my sister's maids, being transported to our desert site at Dunia's request.

When I returned to my tent, I was told by my own maid, Libby, that Kareem, worried when he found our bed empty, had sent her to look for me. After she had assured him that I was safe in the company of Sara, Kareem had taken our daughters on a final camel ride in the desert.

I gratefully took this time to indulge myself in a leisurely bath. Bathing in the desert was no hardship, for our bathrooms were equipped with a small toilet, tiny sink and a large bathtub. During the daylight hours, the desert sun heated the water in large tanks located outside our tents.

After Libby had filled the tub with warm water, I soaked for a short time before attempting to wash the sand from my hair. Afterwards, I prepared myself for what I hoped would be a pleasant last day and night in the desert. I dressed in an ankle-length cotton dress before placing my prayer rug on the carpeted floor of the tent.

After kneeling towards Makkah, I prayed to God that He would maintain my life on a straight course of correct behaviour. My heart and mind then became more peaceful, for I had great hope that I would face the temptations of life with a renewed integrity. Thankfully, at that moment, I had no intimation that a most difficult first test was nearly upon me.

After reading Munira's poem, I was a more subdued Sultana than usual. I needed time to assimilate my thoughts, so when my husband and children invited me to take a short walk in the desert, I refused. When my sisters pleaded with me to join them in a game of backgammon, I declined.

Although I spent that last day in the desert alone, I was not lonely. Preoccupied with my own thoughts, I was a woman who was once again picking up the threads of her life. My inner strength was reinvigorated by a renewed determination to alter the course of my life.

Our family gathering that evening was the most pleasant of all the evenings in the desert, for there was a special poignancy in knowing that the following day would return each of us to the routine of our urban life. When the night's gathering ended under the glittering stars, we warmly embraced each other as we parted to return to our own tents.

Once we were back in our own tent, Kareem and I, and our two daughters, relaxed together. We looked through Polaroid pictures taken on this camping trip. When Amani began to yawn, we decided it was time to retire for the night. I was smiling as Kareem and I went into our bedroom.

Just as I was about to pull my dress over my head to change into a nightgown, I was startled by anguished cries.

Unnerved, I asked Kareem, 'What was *that*?'

Kareem tilted his head as he listened. 'It sounded like the cries of a woman.'

'Oh, Allah! I pray no-one else has been bitten by a snake.'

As the screams became more intense, Kareem grabbed a flashlight and rushed from our tent. I followed him.

The cries had also disturbed Nura and Sara, who along with their husbands, Ahmed and Asad, quickly joined Kareem and me. As we made our way through the labyrinth of the large camp, we saw several of our male employees also bolting from their tents to find the source of the commotion.

The cries slowly faded, but still we followed

the troubling sounds to one of the smaller tents housing our female servants. No light came from within the tent, but loud American rock and roll music suddenly blared into our ears.

Relieved, Kareem muttered, 'Some of the women have gotten into an argument over one thing or another.'

Ahmed nodded. 'Now they are covering up with loud music.'

I felt less certain that all was well. I suggested, 'Since we are here, we should make sure that everyone is all right.'

Sara agreed. 'Yes.'

'And tell them to turn off that music,' Ahmed said with a tinge of annoyance. 'They are disturbing the whole camp.'

While our husbands waited impatiently outside, my sisters and I cautiously entered the tent. The music abruptly ceased.

This tent, which housed ten or more maids, was divided into several private areas by partitions made of heavy fabric. As I parted these drapes, I held Kareem's flashlight high, looking into the women's faces. 'Are you unwell?'

One of the women replied, 'We are fine, ma'am.'

'What has happened?'

Another answered, 'There is no problem, here.'

'Hmmm.' I could tell from the women's expressions and the tone of their voices that they had not been sleeping. Surely these women had heard the loud cries that had travelled the distance to other tents! Yet, no-one offered any information.

I whispered to my sisters. 'They are hiding something.'

'Who is it that we heard screaming?' Nura demanded when we finally came upon Libby.

Libby's eyes were wet with tears, but clearly, she was not the source of the screams we had heard. After hesitating, she looked into my face and whispered, 'Come, ma'am, I will show you.'

Libby was familiar with the interior of this tent and quickly led us through several partitioned areas before pointing at one particular section.

'In there, ma'am,' she whispered before turning and rushing back to her bed.

This was all very strange. By now, our curiosity was even more aroused.

Nura yanked open the partition. I directed the flashlight into the area and was met by a shocking, terrible sight! Two men were assaulting a woman. A third man was watching. Sara screamed.

One man was covering the poor victim's mouth in an effort to silence her cries. Upon seeing us, he now sat like one paralysed. I recognized this man as Taher, the middle son of our sister Tahani.

As if in a slow-motion scene, the second man who was on top of the naked woman gradually turned to face us. I gasped as I recognized Rashed, one of Ali's many sons.

I glanced at the man sitting in the corner of the room, and saw none other than Shadi, Dunia's favoured son. The expression on his face was one of total surprise. He had not anticipated such an intrusion – and certainly not from his aunties.

An enraged Nura shouted, 'What is going on here?'

I cried out, 'Kareem! Come! Quickly!'

Realizing that our husbands were near, my three nephews began to run from the scene, roughly shoving Nura and me aside, and knocking Sara to the ground. I struck one of the three with my flashlight, but was unsuccessful in slowing their frantic retreat. Nura ran after them.

I cried out, 'Kareem! Help us!'

Our husbands apprehended them as the three ran from the tent, and, we heard more shouting.

The small area within the tent suddenly filled with the other female servants. As faint moans came from the woman who had been assaulted, the women gathered round her. I pressed through the crowd of women to see who had been attacked. It was the same young woman whom I had seen earlier in the day with Shadi.

I cried out, 'Our nephews have raped Dunia's maid!'

Sara was suddenly beside me. She began to comfort the distraught girl. 'Poor, poor dear.'

The poor girl had been stripped of her clothing. She lay naked and defenceless before us. Her face was a frightful mask of terror, and her delicate frame was racked with sobs. She was so small that she appeared to be more a child than a woman. I guessed her age to be no more than fifteen or sixteen years.

Libby came into the room and began to soothe her. 'Veena, stop crying. You are safe, now.'

'Bring a pail of water and towels,' Sara ordered. 'She has been seriously injured.'

For the first time I noticed that blood was streaming down the girl's legs onto the Persian carpet.

My fury at this senseless brutality was hard to control. I had a strong desire to attack the attackers, and I stormed outside with that intent.

Our loud cries and shouts had brought all members of our party from their tents. The voices of my sisters, their husbands and sons, along with those of our servants, now merged in a general uproar.

I was pleased to see that Kareem kept a determined grip on Shadi's arm. Asad was grimly holding onto Taher. Ahmed had placed both his arms around Rashed's waist.

Nura tried in vain to speak above the clamour of voices.

Raising my voice as loudly as possible, I, too, tried to explain what had happened.

'A defenceless woman has been assaulted!' I cried out again and again.

Nobody seemed to hear me except Shadi. Our eyes met. The look he gave me was scornful which made me so furious that I seriously considered searching out a heavy stick to beat this nephew of mine!

Ahmed's loud voice of authority finally quieted the crowd. 'Quiet! Everyone!'

After glancing around at the faces in the crowd, Ahmed said, 'The family will meet in my tent. *Now.*'

Pulling the reluctant Shadi along with him, Kareem walked away. I hurried along behind him.

Tahani ran to my side. 'Sultana, whatever has happened?'

I gazed sadly at this sister. Tahani was a wonderful mother, and I knew that she had raised her sons to respect women. Tahani would be devastated to learn of Taher's participation in this terrible attack. I hugged her but said simply, 'We will ask your son for an explanation, Tahani.'

Tahani's eyes lowered in dread of what she was to learn. Dunia, weeping a mother's tears, was trailing along beside Shadi.

Ali was already quietly questioning his son, Rashed. My brother's loud voice suddenly rose in irritation as he exclaimed, 'We were *awakened* for such a thing?'

Ahmed reprimanded him, 'Ali, please do not discuss this business in front of those who are in our employ.'

I glanced behind us. Our curious servants were following us from a short distance.

The moment we entered Ahmed's tent, the clamour rose once again as everyone tried to talk at once. Only after Kareem, shouting angrily, reminded everyone that Ahmed was the eldest in our family, and, as such, deserved to be heard, did the uproar subside.

Ahmed said, 'I do not know what has happened, myself. All I know is that screams coming from the tent of the women awakened us. When our wives went inside to investigate, we heard more screams.'

With his free hand, Ahmed gestured towards Taher, Rashed and Shadi.

'These young men came running from that tent, a place forbidden to them. Shouts from within called out for us to capture the intruders.'

He shrugged. 'And, so we did. How could we know the intruders were our own nephews?'

He nodded in the direction where Nura was standing. 'Nura will have to tell you what happened inside the tent.'

Nura motioned for me to come and stand beside her. With grim determination, I slowly walked across the room and linked arms with my sister. Ali gave me a menacing glare that I ignored.

Nura tried to explain. 'Sultana, Sara and I have witnessed a most horrifying sight.' She nodded towards her nephews. 'These young men whom we all love, were raping a woman. We saw the attack with our own eyes.'

I stared at my nephews in utter contempt. Ali's son, Rashed, was smirking! Dunia's son, Shadi, appeared to be enraged. Of the three, only Taher looked ashamed. His face was red and his chin was hanging against his chest.

Nura continued, 'Not only that, but in their haste to run away, these nephews of ours pushed and shoved their own aunties! Poor Sara was knocked to the ground.'

This was the first Asad had heard of this. Before I had the opportunity to tell him that Sara was unhurt, Asad roughly pushed Taher aside and ran from the tent to look for his wife. Poor Tahani burst into tears. Dunia collapsed against Haifa.

'Who was raped?' Haifa asked.

Nura shrugged. 'I do not know this woman.'

I offered, 'A woman by the name of Veena. She is one of Dunia's maids, I believe.'

For the first time, Shadi spoke in his own defence. His voice was abrupt. 'This woman does not work for my mother. She belongs to me.'

Dunia looked up. 'Shadi is right. The woman is his.'

Shadi's expelled breath was noisy. 'I bought her when I was in Pakistan. She is mine to do with as I please.'

My stomach plummeted. From past knowledge of Ali and his sons, I knew that some of my nephews often travelled to Thailand, the Philippines, India and Pakistan for the purpose of buying time with young prostitutes. But, this was the first time I had heard of any of these nephews actually *purchasing* a woman to bring her into our kingdom as a sexual slave. Certainly, such a thing is not uncommon in Saudi Arabia, and I knew too well that a number of our cousins, such as Faddel, made a habit of such activities, but none of our own husbands or sons had yet descended into such moral decay. At least, not until tonight.

I stared at Shadi in utter loathing. So! My own nephew was a man who would stop at nothing to satisfy his lust!

At this new information, our husbands began to show a certain amount of discomfort. Kareem released his grip on Shadi. Ahmed dropped his arm from Rashed's waist.

Instantly, I knew what our men were thinking. Had Taher, Rashed and Shadi entered the women's tent, which was strictly forbidden to them, and attacked one of our female servants, then they would have seen cause to punish the young men. But now that they had learned that Shadi *owned* the woman who was being attacked, the situation was suddenly viewed in a different manner, no matter how offensive the attack had been. In their eyes, what had happened to Veena was a personal matter between a man and his woman and they had no right to interfere!

Seeing the indignant look on my face, Ahmed said, 'Shadi, the three of you were wrong to shove your aunties! Each of you *will* apologize.'

Shadi's thick lips were tight from anger.

'Yes,' Dunia said. 'I cannot believe that a son of mine would shove my own sisters!'

I turned back to stare in contempt at Dunia. My sister was obviously relieved that our men were now focusing their attention on her son's manners, rather than on his criminal conduct.

'Of course, I apologize,' Shadi said in a sullen tone.

Ali nudged his son.

'And, I apologize, also,' Rashed said with a strained smile.

Although too embarrassed to look into our faces, Taher too mumbled an apology.

At that moment, Sara and Asad came into the tent, and Sara reassured us that she was unhurt.

'Now, apologize once more,' Ali encouraged. 'Your Auntie Sara was nearly injured by your brash act.'

All three young men quickly made their individual apologies to Sara.

Sara ignored them, and searched the crowd until she saw my face. She said, 'Veena has lost too much blood, Sultana. I believe that she needs urgent medical attention.'

I held my hand over my mouth, momentarily speechless at the image that arose in my mind.

No-one spoke until Shadi finally said, 'She is my responsibility. I will take her back into the city.'

I gasped. Unless someone acted, Veena's enslavement would be sanctioned if our family now allowed Shadi to take her away. The subject would be for ever closed. Poor Veena would be used as a sexual toy for Shadi and his friends as long as she was young and attractive. Once they were tired of her, she would become a house servant.

I knew that I could *not* let this unfortunate girl remain in the clutches of my cruel nephew. *Someone* had to take up this helpless woman's cause! Looking around at the faces of my family, I realized that it was up to me. I would have to save this woman!

'No!' I shouted, shocking everyone. 'You will do no such thing, Shadi! Kareem and I will take her to a doctor!'

'Sultana, this is not our business,' Kareem said sternly.

But the tone of my voice silenced Kareem's objections. 'It *is* our business! I do not care how much money Shadi paid for Veena, Kareem. No woman should be the property of any man against her will, and he certainly has no right to rape and abuse her!'

I looked at Sara before turning back to face our men. 'Never again will I stand by while a woman is being abused.' I squared my shoulders in determination. 'If Shadi tries to take this woman away, he will have to kill me first!'

Sara stepped forward and seized my hand. 'Shadi will have to kill me, also.'

Dunia cried out, 'Oh! Allah! Help us!'

Nura pulled me close to her. 'Sultana and Sara are right. We cannot allow a situation that shames Allah Himself.'

Together, Tahani and Haifa walked over to embrace me.

Haifa said, 'I stand with my sisters.'

Tahani's eyes were wet with tears as she stared at her son, Taher. 'Our sons have committed an evil act. I, too, will join Sultana's circle.'

A fierce-looking Ali stared at our husbands,

as he spoke contemptuously. 'You cannot control your women?'

Kareem appeared stricken, but said nothing. Not knowing what to do, Ahmed chose to do nothing.

Only Asad spoke up. 'Our wives are right. We must not support such evil. If our sons need sexual companions, there are many women who will willingly participate. There is no need for our sons to ever take a woman by force.'

The changing situation did not sweeten Shadi's temper. He shouted, 'You are interfering in my business! This woman belongs to me, and there is nothing you can do about it!'

Dunia, who had recovered by now, stood up and rushed to Shadi's side. Standing arm-in-arm with her son, she looked at my sisters and me.

'You are not thinking clearly, sisters. For their health, our sons must have women. Otherwise, there will be a build-up of their body fluids, and this will lead to grave illnesses.'

Nura wearily shook her head at such ignorance. 'You speak nonsense, Dunia.'

Dunia persisted. 'Remember that this woman was purchased from her own father. He received more money than he could ever hope to earn in more than five years! He was *pleased* to sell his daughter! *Pleased*, I tell you! My son did *nothing wrong*!'

I was so disgusted that I could not even look at Dunia, my own sister.

Ali began to speak, 'Dunia is right. Without available women to have sex, our unmarried sons will sicken.'

Asad raised his voice, 'Are we men animals then, Ali?'

Ali then foolishly tried to put the blame on Allah. 'Asad,' he said, 'Great Allah, Himself, made us the way we are.'

At this Ahmed finally burst out, 'Oh, shut up, Ali. You speak as though all men are weak and helpless fools.'

Ali's face grew bright red but the force of Ahmed's words silenced him.

I exchanged a quick look of satisfaction with Sara and began to walk towards the exit of the tent. A battle of wills had begun, and I knew that if I did not prevail, that the life of yet another woman would be destroyed.

I challenged Shadi one last time. 'I am going to Veena, Shadi. If you want her badly enough to kill me, then she is yours.'

'And, me, too,' Sara declared without a moment of hesitation.

'And, me,' Tahani said in a low voice.

'I am coming, too, Sultana,' Haifa called out.

Nura's voice was loud and clear. 'Shadi, your aunties will form a circle of protection around Veena. I advise you not to try to cross it.'

'Sultana's circle of safety,' Tahani said suddenly in a fierce tone.

Apart from Dunia, all my sisters joined me as I left the tent.

Apart from Asad, who quickly followed Sara, our men were left alone, standing in shock.

Epilogue

On that same evening that my sisters and I circled protectively around Veena, our husbands finally moved to support us. Veena was transported to a private medical clinic in Riyadh where her internal injuries were treated. We discovered that she had lost several pints of blood during the gruesome attack. It turned out she was only fourteen years old. Later, after she was deemed medically fit for release from the clinic, my sisters and I learned the details of Veena's pitiful life.

She was born in the slums of Lahore, Pakistan. The family lived in a flimsy shack built from scrap lumber, sheets of metal and cardboard that Veena's parents had gathered from one of Lahore's many city dumps. Her father was a cobbler; her mother, a street beggar.

Veena's childhood had been brutish. She had never been to school, but instead, from the time she could walk, she had been a beggar like her mother.

Other children were born to Veena's parents until the family eventually swelled to twelve. Rarely was there enough food for everyone. Veena could not recall a single instance of eating food until her stomach was full.

In Pakistan, as in Saudi Arabia, there is no value placed on women's lives. Too often, poor families sacrifice their daughters for the general good of the family. And, that is what happened with Veena.

She was always a small, pretty child, and when she reached puberty, her attactiveness was noted by a number of people on the streets and in their slum neighbourhood. Several women known to the family began to tell stories of other pretty young girls who had brought a high price from wealthy brothel keepers who were always looking for new virgins.

Since Veena's family all lived together in one room, she had occasion to observe her father and mother in sexual acts; therefore, she knew the meaning of the women's words. Understanding that she would have no say in her future, though, Veena remained silent.

Soon Veena's beauty was noticed by a man who walked around the city streets observing young female beggars. He sought out Veena's mother and told her that assuming her daughter was still a virgin, there was an opportunity for the family to make a large sum off their daughter's purity. Fearful of contracting AIDS, and other venereal diseases, many wealthy men were looking for young untouched girls. The man offered a small sum as a down payment, promising that if Veena were sold to a rich man, he would return with additional money.

Veena's mother quickly ran to fetch her husband and the three adults agreed upon a price for the hapless Veena.

Veena did recall that her parents both seemed saddened at her departure, but she understood that the money she brought into the family would ensure a year of living well for eleven other people.

She asked for time to say goodbye to her siblings, but the man said he had other transactions to complete, and if Veena did not go with him immediately, that he would cancel the arrangement with her parents. She left with the stranger. Her heart was fluttering in terror, but she steeled herself for the benefit of her younger sisters and brothers.

For over a month, Veena was kept with ten other girls in a small house in Lahore. She was pleased at the opportunity to take frequent baths and to wear decent clothes. For the first time in her life, she received ample food. Veena thought she might like to stay in that house forever. But that was not to be, for various rich men, most of them foreigners, regularly visited the house to look over the available stock of young girls. It was every girl's wish to be purchased by an old man – for it was known that their sexual demands would be less than that of a younger man.

One by one, the other young girls were purchased and taken away. Veena then watched sadly as a number of unhappy girls not chosen by individual clients were transported to brothels in the city. She actually felt herself lucky when she was told that she had been purchased for the pleasure of only one man, a rich man from the Middle East, a man by the name of Shadi.

Veena had never met Shadi, as he had selected her from a book of photographs. He was staying at the home of one of his Pakistani partners, and he had not wanted that man or his family to know that, while in their country, he had purchased a young virgin.

Veena finally came face-to-face with Shadi several days before leaving Lahore. The seller of young girls had taken her to a coffee shop where Shadi could give final approval of his purchase. The meeting was so fleeting that Veena did not exchange a word with her new owner. She was disappointed to see that, indeed, he was a young, strong man. She remembered what the other girls had said about the sexual appetites of young men, and she was frightened. But she had no say in her future. And, too soon, the day arrived that Veena was to depart for ever from her country.

On the plane ride from Pakistan to Saudi Arabia, Shadi's male servants had sat with Veena in coach class, while Shadi remained in first class. Within two hours of their plane landing in Riyadh, Shadi had left for the desert to visit with his parents and other family members. He had taken Veena and several other servants along on the trip with him. Veena claimed that Shadi never once spoke to her on the trip, although she saw him staring at her on several occasions.

Waiting until after the family retired, Shadi had taken his two cousins into Veena's quarters. He had told his two cousins, 'Here is that whore I bought in Pakistan.'

Although Veena had prepared herself to have sex with a man she did not know, she had never imagined that her first sexual experience would be a brutal assault by three strange men.

After being roughly stripped of her clothing, she had been raped first by Shadi. Veena wept as she declared that she had never known such pain! After all, her mother had never screamed during the sexual act with her father. She had no idea that a man's sexual organ was so *big*, and would *hurt* so much.

When she had begun to cry and plead for them to stop, the men had merely laughed and covered her mouth. When the third man climbed on her, Veena truly believed that she was going to die from the assault. And then, miraculously, she was saved. But what was to become of her now?

While my sisters and I wished for nothing more than to send Veena back to her parents, we realized that her family's poverty might once again drive them to sell Veena.

I was the one chosen to tell Veena that it had been decided that she would live in Sara's home, to help my sister care for her younger children. My sisters and I knew that no-one in our family would dare take any action against Sara, for this sister is greatly loved by everyone.

The joy I saw reflected on Veena's face at this news justified every moment of fear and anger I had undergone to free this young woman. Still, my sisters and I were brokenhearted to hear Veena's story, for we knew too well that there were many thousands of similar stories. We sat together for many hours discussing what we might do to stop this ongoing and senseless abuse of innocent women and girls.

During this sad time, the world was shocked by the death of the lovely Diana, Princess of Wales. Princess Diana's death momentarily took our minds away from Veena's cruel life. Several of us had met this extraordinary woman during the years she toured the world as a royal princess. Although none of us could claim to be a close friend of Diana, we had all admired her. Now, we could not imagine such a young and vibrant woman on the way to her grave.

During the days before her funeral, watching the television coverage of her life, I learned much good about this princess that I had not known before. Apparently, no person was too poor or too sick to attract this good woman's attention. And, she was well-known for faithfully following up on her interests with continuing assistance and commitment. In her tremendous kindness and compassion, Princess Diana proved that one person can make a real difference. Every act of kindness generated by this one person resonated as a pebble dropped in water, with ripples which then spread far beyond the original gesture.

This idea flowed so strongly into my mind that I finally began to understand what I might do to help other women. I called my sisters together.

'I suddenly realize the only way we can help women, is to do what we have done with poor Veena,' I said. 'Each time one of us hears of an individual mistreated woman, we will move together to help that one woman in *any* way we can.' I paused. 'We'll create a circle of support.'

Tahani smiled. 'Yes, we will become known as Sultana's circle.'

Haifa expressed her enthusiasm. 'Together, we'll be a great force.'

Sara nodded. 'I have female friends that I can trust. They, too, must begin to seek out women with troubled destinies.'

Nura squeezed my hand. 'Your circle will benefit many women, Sultana.'

Never have I felt more contented with my life, than at that moment.

Following the example of the gentle and loving Princess Diana, I know that this spiral of caring will expand from mother to daughter and down through the chain of life, even reaching through the centuries ahead. My hope is that *every* woman will eventually join my circle, and that every woman in the world will reach out to another woman in need.

And, I pray that the gracious and merciful Allah will bless our mission.

PRINCESS
by Jean Sasson

'Unforgettable . . . fascinating . . . a book to move you to tears'
Fay Weldon

Imagine the life of a Saudi Arabian princess and what do you see? A woman glittering with jewels, living a life of unbelievable luxury. But in reality she lives in a gilded cage. She has no freedom, no vote, no control over her own life, no value but as a bearer of sons. Hidden behind the veil she is a prisoner, her jailers her father, her husband, her sons.

'Sultana' is a member of the Saudi Royal Family, closely related to the King. As she tells of her life – from her turbulent childhood to her arranged marriage – she lifts the veil and reveals a history of appalling oppression and shocking human rights violations such as forced marriages, sex slavery and summary executions.

Princess is a testimony to a woman of indomitable spirit and great courage. By speaking out, 'Sultana' risked her wrath of the Saudi establishment. For this reason, she has told her story anonymously.

A Bantam Paperback
0553 40570 5

DAUGHTERS OF ARABIA
by Jean Sasson

'Women with everything but freedom . . . gripping revelations'
Daily Mail

As second-generation members of the royal family who have benefited from Saudi oil wealth, Maha and Amani have never known the poverty which their parents experienced as children. Surrounded by opulence and luxury from the day they were born, but stifled by the unbearably restricted lifestyle imposed on them, they have reacted in equally desperate ways.

Their dramatic and shocking stories, together with many more which concern other members of Princess Sultana's huge family, are set against a rich backcloth of Saudi Arabian culture and social mores which she depicts with equal colour and authenticity.

A Bantam Paperback
0553 40805 4